The Best

KASHMIRI C

The Best of
KASHMIRI COOKING

Neerja Mattoo

UBSPD

UBS Publishers' Distributors Ltd.

New Delhi • Mumbai • Bangalore • Chennai •
Calcutta • Patna • Kanpur • London

UBS Publishers' Distributors Ltd.
5 Ansari Road, New Delhi-110 002
Phones : 3273601, 3266646 • *Cable* : ALLBOOKS • *Fax* : 3276593, 3274261
e-mail:ubspddel@del3.vsnl.net.in • Internet: www.ubspd.com
10 First Main Road, Gandhi Nagar, Bangalore-560 009
Phones : 2263901, 2263902, 2253903 • *Cable* : ALLBOOKS • *Fax* : 2263904
6, Sivaganga Road, Nungambakkam, Chennai-600 034
Phones : 8276355, 8270189 • *Cable* : UBSIPUB • *Fax* : 8278920
8/1-B, Chowringhee Lane, Calcutta-700 016
Phones : 2441821, 2442910, 2449473 • *Cable* : UBSIPUBS • *Fax* : 2450027
e-mail:ubspdcal@calvsnl.net.in
5 A, Rajendra Nagar, Patna-800 016
Phones : 672856, 673973, 656170 • *Cable* : UBSPUB • *Fax* : 656169
80, Noronha Road, Cantonment, Kanpur-208 004
Phones : 369124, 362665, 357488 • *Fax* : 315122

Distributors for Western India:
M/s Preface Books
Shivali Apartments, Plot No. 1, S. No. 25/4, Chintamani Society,
Karve Nagar, Pune 411052 • Phone: 346203

Overseas Contact
475 North Circular Road, Neasden, London NW2 7QG
Tele : 081-450-8667 • *Fax* : 0181-452-6612 Attn: UBS

First Published	**1995**
First Reprint	**1996**
Second Reprint	**1999**

Cover Design : UBS Art Studio

Typeset by S.J.I. Services, New Delhi
Printed at Nutech Photolithographers, Delhi

To
my mother

Contents

Introduction

Kashmir, the valley spread between the Himalayan and the Pir Panjal Ranges, has had a turbulent history. Its people have perfected the art of surviving in harsh circumstances, making the most of whatever is available, and learning to value the good things of life. Living in what is perhaps the most beautiful place in the world has also developed their aesthetic sense.

Whether engaged in embroidering a shawl, painting a papier mache vase or cooking a meal, the Kashmiris' natural talent helps them achieve the exacting standards they set for themselves. With the added ingredients of love, care and patience, each production becomes a work of art.

Snow-bound for much of the year and confined to the house during bleak wintry days, the Kashmiris developed an almost obsessive interest in food — it could bring enjoyment and sparkle to life, even on the dreariest of days. Great care is taken to plan and prepare a meal, and all social activity revolves around well-cooked food. Kashmiri food includes dishes of mutton, fish, chicken, wild fowl and all the delectable vegetables and fruits — fresh and dried — which Kashmir is famous for, and which have delicious flavors, unmatched in the world.

Raising the culinary art to a high level of sophistication, Kashmiri cuisine has acquired an almost legendary reputation. Situated at the crossroads of cultural currents from the Middle East, Central Asia, the East and the South, in Kashmiri kitchens we find a blend of the best elements of Indian, Iranian, Afghan and Central Asian *haute cuisine*. This culminates in the celebrated Kashmiri 'Wazawan'— literally, the grand bazaar of cooks — which is the traditional Muslim feast, consisting of dozens of meat and a few vegetable dishes.

One of the most striking aspects of this cuisine is its great variety and range for all seasons and occasions. Even the humblest of vegetables is transformed into a delicacy through a subtle combination of spices. Powdered dry ginger and fennel are the main spices which go into Kashmiri cooking to give it the exotic flavors, distinct from other Indian food.

The use of the fleshy, flavorsome, but not too hot, red chilies grown in Kashmir is also responsible for giving some dishes a taste and color all their own. The deep, pinkish-maroon color of some dishes comes from using the extract from the flowers of a variety of celosia, popularly known as cocks-comb. Saffron, which grows in Kashmir, is also used generously. Yoghurt is an important ingredient in a number of dishes. Mustard oil is the main cooking medium, though 'ghee' (clarified butter) is also used in some preparations.

There have been many occasions when non-Kashmiris, licking their fingers after an unforgettable culinary experience in Kashmiri households, ask to be told the secrets of cooking which provides such relish, pleasure and excitement to the palate. This book is meant to help them recapture the magic in their own kitchens. Over hundreds of years of experiment and refinement, Muslim and Hindu (Kashmiri Pandit) cooks (both professionals and home cooks) have honed their skills to evolve non-vegetarian and vegetarian dishes. It is these recipes, which have been collected over the years, that form the content of this book.

Wazawan Delicacies

'Wazawan' is the term used for the traditional Kashmiri Muslim feast which is entirely non-vegetarian — even the vegetables are cooked in meat-stock. In fact, enormous quantities of meat are boiled for a length of time and this stock, rich in juices, is used to make up the gravy for the great variety of dishes. Wazawan is an elaborate meal served and eaten in so ceremonial a manner that it is like a ritual conducted according to its own strict rules. The multi-course meal is cooked by professional cooks (the Kashmiri term for a cook is 'Waza'). The guests take their seats on the carpeted floor in long rows, facing each other across long, narrow white sheets spread on the floor. Two people, one carrying an intricately engraved copper basin with an attached soap dish, known as a 'tush', and the other a shapely jug called a 'naar', come before each guest so that he can wash his hands before eating. The meal is then served in large, tinned copper platters, covered with dome-like lids. All the metal vessels are beautiful, yet completely functional. When all the guests have a platter — four people eat from each platter — placed before them, the lids are lifted simultaneously to reveal a mound of rice, visible through a tracery of four portions of a number of dishes arranged all over it — seekh kebab, dum kokur, methimaaz and tabakh maaz. As the guests begin to eat, the wazas arrive on the scene, balancing enormous vessels on their hips. With long-handled ladies, they serve the other wazawan delicacies one by one according to a strict order. Rista is followed by roghanjosh, danival korma, tsaman, martsawangan korma, aabgosh, alubukhara maaz, bumtsoomth khanji or any other seasonal vegetable, and goshtaba, in that order. Pulao, zarda, a number of chutneys, onions dipped in hot vinegar sauce, thin slivers of radish and plain yoghurt in earthenware bowls are served as side dishes. When the meal is over, hands are washed again. Phirin in summer and halwa in winter are served as dessert to bring this extraordinary culinary experience to an end.

Apart from being a feast served at weddings, festivals like Id, thanks-giving after a safe return from the Haj pilgrimage or other celebrations, wazawan is an essential part of dinner-diplomacy in Kashmir! Mellowed after the shared meal with its surfeit of sensuous joys, even adversaries find themselves filled with the 'milk of human kindness' and the animosities disappear. No wonder Kashmiris long for wazawan and its ambience — peace, goodwill and general well-being.

The dishes given here can easily be prepared at home, if the recipes are followed faithfully. The only equipment which would, perhaps, be unfamiliar are a stone slab known as 'goshiphor' and a wooden mallet and pestle which are required for certain preparations. The authentic flavors and results cannot be achieved with a mixer-grinder or a food processor.

Seekh Kabab
(Barbecued Mince Rolls)

Ingredients (Serves 8)

2 pounds ground beef or lamb
4 black cardamoms, crushed coarsely
½ tsp. black cumin
¼ tsp. sugar
1 tsp. fennel powder
2 tsp. dry ginger powder
2 tbsp. ghee (clarjfied butter)
2 onions
4 tomatoes

Preparation

Mix all the ingredients (except onions and tomato) well and divide into 16 portions. Taking a skewer in one hand, wrap one portion of mince all round it. Press and smooth with your hand to cover about 15 cm (6 inches) of the skewer. Grill over a charcoal fire (or in a grill), turning around frequently till browned all around. When done, dip your hand in cold water and push the kabab off the skewer. When all the kababs are done, lightly fry in a frying pan. Arrange in a shallow dish and garnish with lightly-fried onion and tomato slices. Serve hot with mint chutney.

Gushtaba

Seekh Kebab

Rista

Roghan Josh

Kokur

Tsamun Kaliya

Nadur Yakhni

TABAKHMAAZ/KABARGAH
(Tender Fried Ribs)

Ingredients (Serves 8)

3 cups milk
½ cup water
1 cup yoghurt
2 pounds fatty mutton (from the ribs). Cut into 3-rib pieces about 4 inches (10 cms) long.
3 bay leaves
1 tsp. salt
1 tsp. ginger powder
1½ tsp. fennel powder
1 tsp. finely chopped ginger
¼ tsp. asafoetida-water
2 cups yoghurt
4 cloves
2 black cardamoms
3 green cardamoms crushed
1 inch stick of cinnamon
2 tsp. white cumin seed
(cloves, black cardamoms, green cardamoms, cinnamon, white cumin seed:) *Grind to a fine powder.*
1 cup ghee (clarified butter)
silver leaf (3 or 4)

Preparation

Bring the milk, water, and 1 cup yoghurt to a boil. Add the mutton, the bay leaves, salt and spices. Cover and cook on gentle heat till the meat is tender. If any liquid remains, raise the heat and dry it up. Cool to room

Contd. ...

temperature. Whisk the 2 cups yoghurt well in a shallow bowl, adding the ground spices. Dip the mutton pieces in the yoghurt so that each piece is well coated. Heat ghee in a 'wok' or 'karhai' and deep fry two or three pieces at a time, to a rich brown colour. Arrange on a pre-heated dish, sprinkle a little garam masala while still hot and coat each piece with silver leaf. Serve sizzling hot.

Dum Kokur
(Pot Roasted Chicken)

Ingredients (Serves 4)

1 tsp. salt
1 tsp. turmeric powder
1½ tsp. red chili powder
1½ tsp. fennel powder
1 whole clove garlic. Peel and grind into a paste.
1 small piece ginger. Grate fine
2 tbsp. yoghurt
1 large chicken. Pluck feathers and clean the inside. Do not remove skin. Cut into good sized pieces.
½ cup ghee
3 cloves
1 large onion. Slice fine.
¼ tsp. cumin. Crush.
2 black cardamoms. Crush.

Preparation

Mix salt, turmeric, chili powder, fennel powder, garlic and ginger in yoghurt and rub the paste well on the chicken pieces. Leave in a dish for 3 hours, covered. Heat ghee in a thick-bottomed pan. Drop the cloves in. When sizzling, add the onions and fry till golden brown. Add cummin and cardamom. Now put in the chicken along with the juices that would have collected in the dish. Toss them around for one minute. Cover with a tight-fitting lid and simmer on low heat for an hour, by which time the chicken should be tender and nicely browned.

Rista
(Mince Paste Balls in Xed Gravy)

Ingredients (Serves 8)

¼ pound dried cockscomb flower-heads
2 pounds mutton (hind leg is best)
1 teaspoon lumps of mutton fat
2 tsp. salt
2 tsp. ginger powder
3 tsp. red chili powder
4 black cardamoms
½ tsp. cumin seeds
1½ tsp. turmeric powder
5 green cardamoms
1 stick cinnamon
3 cloves
½ cup oil
2 medium onions, chopped fine
3 tsp. red chili powder
2 tsp. garam masala

Preparation

Boil the cockscomb flower-heads in 1 cup water and squeeze out through a piece of muslin cloth to extract the purple-coloured juice.

Remove the bones from the meat and pound on a stone slab with a wooden mallet, gradually adding the lumps of fat with a little water, 1 tsp. salt, 1 tsp. ginger and 1½ tsp. fennel powder, black cardamom seeds and cumin. Keep pounding till the mutton is reduced to an absolutely fine, sticky paste free from any granular lumps. Wet your palms and form into balls the size of a golf ball (about 2 cm in diameter). Boil 6 cups of water, add 1 tsp. salt, turmeric powder, crushed green cardamoms, cinnamon, cloves. Put in the mince balls (ristas) one by one and allow to cook till spongy to the touch. While the ristas are cooking, heat oil in a deep skillet. Brown the onions in it. Remove with a slotted spoon and grind to a smooth brown paste. While the oil is still hot but removed from heat, add the chili powder and cockscomb flower juice, 1 tsp. ginger and 2 tsp. fennel powder. The oily liquid should now have a rich red color. Pour it on the ristas along with the onion paste and cook for another 15 minutes on low heat, taking care that the gravy does not dry up. Sprinkle the garam masala and remove from heat after five minutes. Serve hot.

Dani

(Marrow-Bone in Gravy)

Ingredients (Serves 8)

4 cups water
2 pounds medium-sized marrow bones along with the meat around them from the leg and the shoulder
2 tsp. ginger powder
3 tsp. fennel powder
1½ tsp. turmeric powder
2 tsp. salt
3 cloves
1 stick cinnamon
4 black cardamoms
5 green cardamoms
2 medium onions, chopped fine
5 tbsp. oil
3 tsp. red chili powder
¼ pound dried cockscomb flower-heads. Boil in a little water and strain out the liquid through a piece of muslin.
½ tsp. black cumin
2 tsp. garam masala

Preparation

Bring the water to a boil. Put in the meat with ginger, fennel, turmeric powder, salt, cloves, cinnamon and cardamom. Cook till tender. Meanwhile, fry the onions in oil till they are rich brown. Remove with a slotted spoon and grind to a fine paste. While the oil is still hot, but removed from heat, add the red chili powder and cockscomb flower juice. Stir well, add ½ tsp. black cumin and bring to a boil. Pour over the marrow bones. When the mutton is tender and the gravy reduced to just about a cup, add the onion paste and garam masala. Simmer for five minutes. Serve on a plate of rice.

MARTSAWANGAN KORMA

(Mutton in Chili Sauce)

Ingredients (Serves 8)

8 large red Kashmiri chilies
$^1/_3$ cup of ghee
2 onions, chopped fine
3 cloves
2 pounds mutton chops or cuts from the leg in largish pieces
1½ tsp. salt
2 tsp. ginger powder
4 black cardamoms
5 green cardamoms
1 stick cinnamon
3 bay leaves
2 tsp. garam masala

Preparation

Boil the de-seeded red chilies in 2 cups of water till they are quite soft. Cool and rub through a piece of soft muslin, squeezing out all the pulp and juice. Keep aside. Heat oil in a thick-bottomed pan. When smoking, add onions and stir fry till golden brown. Now add the cloves, mutton and salt. Stir, turning all the pieces well. Lower the heat. Keep stirring and turning the pieces till the liquid is absorbed and the mutton evenly browned. Now add spoonfuls of the chili juice, turning the mutton frequently so that it does not stick to the bottom of the pan. When all the chili juice has been used up and the meat a dark maroon in color, add 2 cups of water, ginger powder, crushed cardamoms, cinnamon and bay leaves. Simmer till the meat is tender and the gravy thick. Sprinkle garam masala and remove from heat. Serve hot.

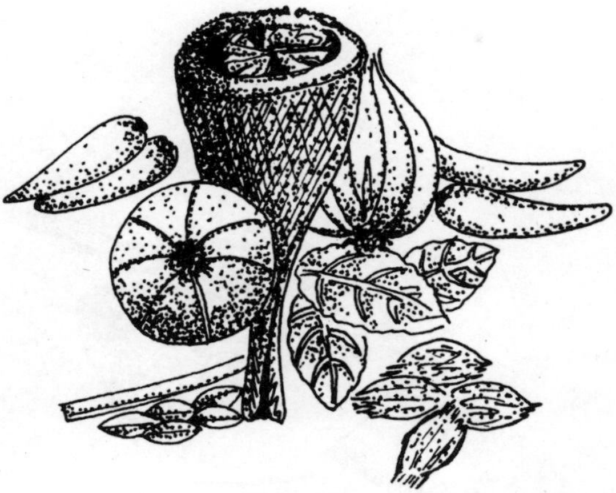

ALUBUKHARAMAAZ
(Quince and Lamb Curry)

The procedure for this dish is the same as that for Martsawangan Korma, with the difference that to 2 pounds of lamb is added ½ pound of dried quince slices which have been softened by soaking in hot water for one hour, while it is simmering.

Danival Korma

(Mutton with Coriander)

Ingredients (Serves 8)

¼ cup oil
2 pounds mutton. Cut into medium-sized pieces.
1 cup chopped onion. Grind to a paste.
2 cups yoghurt. Whisk well.
$^1/_3$ cup green coriander. Wash, clean and chop coarsely.
10 green cardamoms. Crush.

Preparation

Heat oil in a thick-bottomed vessel. Add the meat and onion paste. Stir well. Cover with a lid and allow to cook for 10 minutes. Stir again. The color at this stage should be a very light golden brown. Add the yoghurt while stirring so that the mutton is well coated. Reduce heat and cook till tender. It may be necessary to add a little water, as the dish must have some gravy. Stir in the chopped coriander and cardamoms. Cover and cook for another 2 minutes. Serve hot.

TSAMUN

(Cottage Cheese in Tomato Sauce)

Ingredients (Serves 8)

2 pounds fresh home-made cottage cheese, firm to the touch. Cut into thick slices about 4 cms x 4 cms x 1 cm.
½ cup oil
4 cups stock or water
3 cloves
2 onions. Slice, fry till brown and liquidise
2 tablespoons masala vari (Kashmiri Spice-Cake)
2 level tsp. red chili powder
1½ tsp. salt
3 pounds tomatoes. Blanch and remove seeds
5 green cardamoms
1 tsp. ginger powder
2 level tsp. garam masala
2 bay leaves

Preparation

Deep fry the thick slices of cheese in oil till golden brown. Drain and put into the slightly-warmed stock or water. Leave about ¼ cup of oil in the vessel. Add the cloves, onion paste, masala vari, chili powder, salt and crushed tomatoes together. Stir-fry on medium heat till a thick, smooth sauce is formed. Add the cheese slices along with the stock/water, crushed cardamoms, ginger powder, garam masala and bay leaves. Simmer till the gravy is thick, the cheese spongy and the oil swims on the surface.

AABGOSH

(Mutton in Milky Gravy)

Ingredients (Serves 8)

2 pounds mutton (tail, or ribs or shoulder, with fat)
1 black cardamom
1 stick cinnamon
3 tsp. fennel powder
6 cloves
3 cloves garlic
2 cm ginger, finely sliced
1½ tsp. salt
1 onion, sliced
1 shallot, sliced
4 cups milk
4 green cardamoms

Preparation

Boil 3 cups water. Put in the mutton, crushed black cardamom, cinnamon, 1½ tsp. fennel, 2 cloves crushed garlic, ginger, 1½ tsp. salt. Cook till the mutton is tender. Strain the gravy. Remove the mutton pieces. Heat 4 to 6 tbsp. ghee. Stir fry the onion and shallot till golden. Remove with a slotted spoon, drain in order to crisp it and pound to a paste. Pour the oil on the mutton and gravy. Add 4 cups thickened milk and simmer. Add 1 tsp. of gravy to the onion paste and pour into the gravy. Put in cinnamon and 1 tsp. fennel powder. Simmer till the gravy is reduced to about 3 cups. Put in crushed green cardamoms just before removing from heat.

Bamtsoonthi Khanji
(Spicy Quince)

Ingredients (Serves 8)

6 large quince
$^1/_3$ cup oil
2 cloves
1½ tsp. chili powder
1 tsp. turmeric powder
1 inch piece of masala vari (the garlic based kind)
1½ tsp. ginger powder
2½ tsp. fennel powder
1 black cardamom
1 tsp. salt

Preparation

Peel, core and quarter the quince, i.e., cut each quince lengthwise into 4 pieces. Fry in batches in hot oil till reddish brown in color. Drain and keep aside. Heat 3 tbsp. oil and put in the cloves. Remove from heat and put in chili and turmeric powder, masala vari and ½ cup of water together. Bring to a boil. Gently put in the quince pieces. Add 1 cup of water and the rest of the spices. Simmer till most of the water is absorbed. Serve hot.

GOSHTABA

(Mince-Paste Balls in Yoghurt Gravy)

Ingredients (Serves 4)

2 pounds mutton, pounded to a paste
1 tablespoon lumps of mutton fat, pounded to a paste
2 tsp. ginger powder
3 tsp. fennel powder
4 black cardamoms
½ tsp. cumin seeds
¼ cup oil
¼ cup ghee
2 medium-sized onions, finely chopped
4 cups yoghurt. Whisk thoroughly
2 tsp. dry mint powder. (Mint leaves should be dried in the sun and then pounded to a fine powder. Sieve.)
5 green cardamoms
2 tsp. garam masala
3 cloves
1 stick cinnamon

Preparation

Pound the meat and fat to as fine a paste as that for ristas, adding 1 tsp. ginger powder, 1½ tsp. fennel powder, 2 black cardamom seeds, 1½ tsp. cumin, and 1 tsp. salt. Form into balls almost twice the size of ristas (about 6 cm diameter). Boil 6 cups of water and put in the Goshtabas and allow to cook till spongy. (Almost all the water should have evaporated by

Contd. ...

the time this stage is reached). While the Goshtabas are cooking, heat oil in a thick-bottomed vessel. When smoking, add the ghee. Put in the finely-chopped onions. Stir-fry on medium heat till light golden (not brown) in color. Remove with a slotted spoon and grind to a fine paste. Meanwhile, pour the well-whisked yoghurt and 1 tsp. salt into the slightly-cooled oil-ghee, stirring vigorously. Put the vessel back on the stove and let it boil, stirring all the time. Put the spongy Goshtabas into the yoghurt gravy. Add 1 tsp. ginger and 1½ tsp. fennel powder, cumin, mint powder, garam masala and crushed green and black cardamoms, 1 cup water and the onion paste. Add cloves and cinnamon. Allow to simmer for one hour before serving. The gravy should be thick.

Non-Vegetarian Specialities of the Kashmiri Pandits

Kashmiri Pandits, unlike most Brahmins elsewhere, are not vegetarian. In fact, non-vegetarian dishes are an essential part of some of the rituals and ceremonies during the Shivratri and Navreh celebrations, much to the surprise, and even horror, of other Brahmins in the rest of the country!

Apparently the guardian spirit of the household and other mischievous spirits need to be kept in good humour during the long, bleak days of winter and that can only be done by offerings of specially-cooked fish, fowl and mutton. The *Yaksha* demands whole lentils and rice cooked in ghee and garnished with fish, mutton and pickles on the night of the new moon in mid-winter known as 'khetsi mavas'! Nothing less than hot fish curry will do for the presiding spirit of the home for whom the mistress of the house has to carry a mouth-watering platter to the attic at least once in the winter season.

A pilgrimage to Hari Parbat — the shrine on the hill of that name in Srinagar — always meant gorging on turmeric rice soaked in the chili gravy of hot, curried cubes of liver. For the youngsters in the family the most exciting part of Shivratri festivities is the menu—fish, lotus stem, wild duck, and mutton cooked in different ways for the occasion. All one's Muslim friends and neighbours joined in the feast the day after the night of the *puja*. A dish of vosta hak, a delicate, rare vegetable which only grows in Kashmir in early spring is essential to the festive meal cooked for Navreh—the Kashmiri Pandit New Year in spring. The onionless dahl cooked for the meal served at the conclusion of a Yagneopavit havan (the sacred thread ceremony of Brahmins) has an unforgettable taste and flavor. Incidentally, this and the meal served at the bride's home just before the wedding ceremony begins are purely vegetarian feasts.

The Kashmiri Pandit cuisine has grown with the religious and cultural practices of this sub-culture. Traditionally, onions and garlic are taboo; and even today, while cooking festive food, they are not used. Asafoetida is preferred instead for its strong flavor. Hence the flavor of meat dishes cooked in Kashmiri Pandit households is quite different from that of the Wazawan.

Roghanjosh
(Browned Mutton)

Ingredients (Serves 8)

2 pounds mutton (preferably leg), cut into large pieces. Chops will also do.
1½ tbsp. yoghurt (dahi)
4 large Kashmiri red chilies
1 tsp. nutmeg, 2 dry dates
½ tsp. sugar
8 tbsp. oil
3 cloves
2 tsp. asafoetida-water
1½ tsp. salt
2 tsp. dry ginger powder
3 tsp. fennel powder
3 black cardamoms
1 medium stick cinnamon
1 tbsp. ghee

Preparation

Wash the mutton and pat it dry. Spread the pieces on a large platter and rub the yoghurt in thoroughly. Keep aside for half an hour. Boil the red chilies in one cup of water till soft. When cool, rub the chilies through a piece of muslin and squeeze out the pulp and juice. Strain and keep aside. Pound the dates, sugar and nutmeg to make as fine a powder as

Contd. ...

possible. Heat oil in a thick-bottomed pan. When it has been smoking for about 3 minutes, add the cloves, mutton, asafoetida-water and salt—in that order. Stir, turning all the pieces well. Lower heat. Cover the pan for a few minutes.

Continue the procedure of alternate stirring and covering, turning all the pieces over frequently, till all the water is absorbed and the mutton pieces are all evenly browned.

At this stage, begin to add spoonfuls of the red chili juice while continuing to stir. Care must be taken to ensure that nothing clings to the bottom and all the chili juice is used up. Sprinkle the date-sugar-nutmeg powder. Add 2 cups hot water, ginger, fennel powder and crushed cardamoms. Add cinnamon stick. Cover and simmer till the meat is tender, the water absorbed and the oil floating on the surface.

Pour the hot ghee over the meat and sprinkle with garam masala. Cover and cook for 2 minutes. Gently shake the pan and remove from the heat. Serve hot. A few blanched almonds may be used as garnishing.

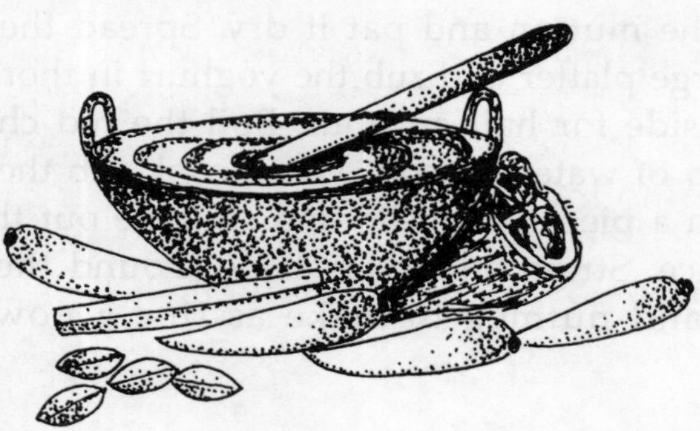

KALIYA

(Mutton in Yellow Gravy)

Ingredients (Serves 8)

2 pounds mutton. Cut into medium-sized pieces. (An even mixture of fatty and lean meat from the breast and shoulder is a good idea.)
5 cloves
1½ tsp. salt
2 large bay leaves
1½ tsp. dry turmeric powder
½ tsp. asafoetida-water (dissolve ¼ teaspoon in a little water)
2 tsp. dry ginger powder
3 tsp. dry fennel powder
¼ cup yoghurt
2 black cardamoms
5 green cardamoms
4 tbsp. oil
A pinch of saffron

Preparation

Bring 2 cups water to a boil. Add the mutton, cloves, salt, bay leaves, turmeric and asafoetida-water. Boil for 10 minutes, without covering. Stir the ginger and fennel powder into the yoghurt till smooth. Pour over the boiling meat. Stir well. Add coarsely ground cardamoms. Cover with a tight-fitting lid. Simmer till

Contd. ...

the mutton is tender and the liquid reduced to half. The gravy should be the consistency of very thin sauce. Heat oil, and pour sizzling hot on the mutton. Simmer for 10 minutes more. Add garam masala and the saffron, crushed and dissolved in water. Simmer for 5 minutes. Remove from heat and serve hot.

Kofta
(Mince Rolls)

Ingredients (Serves 8 to 12)

1 tsp. dry ginger powder
1 tsp. fennel powder
3 black cardamoms
3 black peppercorns. Grind coarsely.
1 tsp. black cumin seeds
2 pounds minced mutton. (Ask the butcher to chop the meat from a leg into a very fine mince, sprinkling a little salt on it.)
1 tsp. red chili powder
¼ tsp. sugar
2 tsp. gram flour
1 tsp. yoghurt or one egg
A pinch of baking soda or baking powder

For the gravy:

5 tbsp. oil
1 large onion (sliced fine)
3 cloves
1 tsp. red chili powder
1 tbsp. yoghurt
1 tsp. dry ginger powder
2 tsp. fennel powder
½ tsp. salt

Preparation

Mix all the spices, except the red chili powder, thoroughly into the mince and keep aside. Heat 2 tbsp. oil till it smokes. Toss the onions in. Reduce heat. Stir fry till the onions are a rich brown color. Strain out and keep aside. Make a slight depression in the mince. Lay the red chili powder and sugar in a heap in it and quickly pour the sizzling hot oil (in which the onions were fried) over it. Add the gram flour, yoghurt or egg and the baking soda. Knead the mince thoroughly. Now divide into about 30 portions. Wet your palms. Take a portion and press into a ball in your palms. Now rub the palms together so that the ball is rolled into a smooth cylinder about 3 inches (8 cm) long and 1 inch (3 cm) in diameter. These are the koftas.

Heat 5 tbsp. oil in a thick-bottomed vessel. When it smokes, add the cloves. Mix the red chili powder in the yoghurt. Pour into the hot oil, stirring well. Add ½ tsp asafoetida-water. Cook for 2 minutes. Put in one litre (5 or 6 cups) water. When it boils, add the ginger and fennel powder and salt. Gently lower the koftas into it, turning the vessel this way and that till the gravy coats the koftas and they begin to swell and turn pale in color. Do not stir, otherwise the koftas will crack or break up. Sprinkle the fried onions over and cover the vessel with a tight-fitting lid. Simmer on gentle heat till the koftas are soft to the touch, all the water absorbed and the oil floats on the surface. Just before removing from the heat, add a tsp. of garam masala. Garnish with a few coarsely-ground green cardamoms and blanched almond halves. Serve hot.

Alu Bukhara Kofte

(Plum Stuffled Mince Balls)

Prepare the minced meat exactly as for plain koftas. Soak dried plums in cold water for half an hour to soften them and remove the pit carefully. Before rolling the minced meat into a kofta, place a dried plum and a blanched almond in the center. Form into a smooth round ball. Cook in gravy, just like for plain koftas.

Shami — (Kashmiri Pandit Style)

(Mince Slices in Yoghurt Gravy)

Ingredients (Serves 8)

2 pounds minced meat. (Ideally, ask the butcher to finely chop fatty mutton from the leg or shoulder with a sprinkling of salt, on his chopping board. Afterwards pound it well in a mortar at home.)
3 black cardamoms, coarsely crushed
2 green cardamoms
½ tsp. white cumin powder (freshly ground)
1 tsp. dry ginger powder
1½ tsp. dry fennel powder
⅓ tsp. sugar
1 pinch baking soda or baking powder
½ tsp. salt

For the gravy:

2 cups yoghurt
1 tsp. ginger powder
2 tsp. fennel powder
4 cloves
1 tsp. salt
3 bay leaves

Preparation

Mix all the ingredients in the mince. Knead thoroughly. Form into 4 rolls, rounded at the ends. Wet your palms before doing this.

Boil 1½ cups water. Gently drop in the rolls. Cook till spongy to the touch. Remove from the heat. Allow to cool to room temperature. Lift the rolls out on a board and slice into 1½-cm thick slices, like bread. Keep aside.

For the gravy, take 2 cups of yoghurt in a thick-bottomed vessel. Whisk thoroughly, adding a little warm stock (in which the mince rolls had been cooked). Boil, stirring all the time. Add 1 tsp. of dry ginger, powder, 2 tsp. fennel powder, 4 cloves, 1 tsp. salt, 3 bay leaves. Keep stirring all the time so that it does not curdle. Gently add the shami slices. Cook till the gravy is as thick as pouring custard consistency and the shami is spongy.

Heat 3 tbsp. ghee and pour it sizzling hot on the shami. Add 1 tsp. garam masala. Cover and simmer for 3 minutes. The oil should rise to the surface by this time. Remove from heat and serve hot.

KOFTA YAKHNI
(Mince Balls in Yoghurt Gravy)

Ingredients (Serves 8 to 12)

As for Shami

Preparation

Follow the procedure for mince as for Shami, but form the mince into small round balls the size of large cherries. The preparation of gravy and the method of cooking one the same as for Shami.

YAKHNI
(Mutton in Yoghurt Gravy)

Ingredients (Serves 8)

2 pounds mutton (ribs or other fatty mutton cut into medium-size pieces)
1½ tsp. salt
4 cloves
2 bay leaves
2 black cardamoms, crushed coarsely
2 tsp. ginger powder
3 tsp. fennel powder
4 cups yoghurt, whisked well
4 tablespoons oil or ghee
4 green cardamoms, crushed coarsely
1 tsp. garam masala

Preparation

Bring 1½ cups of water to boil in a pan. Put in the mutton, salt, cloves, bay leaves, black cardamom, ginger and fennel powder. Cover and cook till the mutton is tender.

Whisk the yoghurt well, adding a little hot gravy from the mutton to make it warm. Pour the yoghurt over the meat, stirring all the time till it comes to the boil. Keep stirring, while simmering, to make the gravy tnto a smooth thin custard-like consistency. One or two tsp. of cornstarch may be added to thicken,

Contd. ...

if the gravy appears to be too thin after it has been simmering for about 15 minutes. (The cornstarch must first be made into a smooth paste with a little cold water). Heat the oil or ghee and pour sizzling hot on the mutton. Sprinkle 1 tsp. garam masala. Sprinkle with crushed green cardamom. Cover again. After 2 minutes, remove from heat. Serve hot.

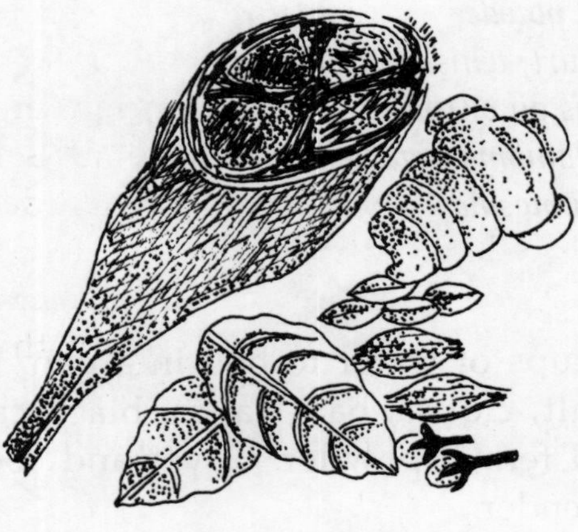

Vegetarian Food

Kashmir has a climate in which almost all the vegetables known to the world grow in abundance. In addition, there is the green leafy one known as 'hak' that is available throughout the year. The cold winters, with their snow and frost, not only seem to enhance the content and flavor of the leaf, but also cause it to cook faster, allowing it to retain its bright green color.

Kashmiris believe that the vegetables that grow with organic manure in their 'floating gardens' have a taste, flavor and content superior to any found elsewhere. And if you happen to taste them, you will perhaps agree. Lotus stem grows in the shallow backwaters of the Dal, Wular and Anchar lakes. It is a very popular vegetable and provides excellent roughage. Some of the festivals of Kashmiri Pandits demand at least one dish of lotus stem as part of the ritual, even if in combination with mutton, fish, or fowl!

Dum Aloo

(Browned Potatoes)

Ingredients (Serves 8)

2 pounds potatoes (choose shapely, round, medium-sized, firm ones)
3 cups oil
4 cloves
2 tsp. asafoetida water
1 tsp. salt
2 tsp. red chili powder
2 tbsp. yoghurt
2 black cardamoms
1 tsp. chopped ginger
1 tsp. ginger powder
2 tsp. fennel powder
½ tsp. black cumin seeds (shahi zeera)
Garam masala

Preparation

Wash the potatoes well. Boil till soft, but firm. They should not crack or become too soft, but ensure that they are done to the core. A good test is to pierce the potato with a thin toothpick — it should pass through without resistance, while the potato remains whole and does not crumble in your hand. Peel and pierce each potato with a toothpick from side to side and top to bottom, right through.

Heat the oil in a deep frying pan or wok. Deep fry the potatoes in batches, till evenly browned. Reduce the heat occasionally while turning the potatoes to ensure they do not burn or you can also sprinkle a little water to reduce the temperature of the oil, so that the potatoes are a rich, deep, reddish-brown color. Remove with a slotted spoon, drain and keep aside. Pour about 8 tbsp. of the oil into a thick-bottomed pan and add the cloves, asafoetida water and salt. Take off the heat and put in chili powder and yoghurt, one after the other, but almost simultaneously. Put the pan back on the heat, stirring well. As the yoghurt curdles and becomes somewhat crumbly and the color of the oil is a dark (but not burnt) red, add asafoetida-water, 2 cups water, the crushed cardamom, ginger and fennel powder. When boiling, put in the fried whole potatoes. Cover with a lid and cook on gentle heat till all the water is absorbed and the oil floats on top. Press the cumin in your palms, rubbing them together and sprinkle on top. The potatoes should have become soft, but still remain whole. Finish off with a sprinkling of garam masala before removing from heat. Serve hot.

TSAMAN

(Cottage Cheese in Yellow Gravy)

Ingredients (Serves 8 to 10)

2 pounds (32 ounces) cottage cheese, cut into cubes 5 cm × 5 cm × 2 cm.
1½ cups oil
1 tsp. salt
2 tsp. dry ginger powder
1¼ tsp. turmeric
5 tsp. dry fennel powder
4 cloves
3 green cardamoms (crushed)
1 black cardamom (crushed)
3 bay leaves
½ cup milk
1.tsp. garam masala

Preparation

Deep fry the cheese cubes in oil in batches till golden. Drain and put into a vessel containing 2 cups of salted boiling water. Add the ginger, turmeric and fennel powder, cloves, cardamoms and bay leaves. While boiling, pour in the milk. Cover and cook till the gravy is reduced to half. Heat 4 tbsp. oil. Pour sizzling hot over the cheese. Sprinkle the garam masala over and remove from heat. Serve hot.

Hak
(Kashmiri Greens)

Ingredients (Serves 8 to 10)

2 pounds green hak (These are large, green, wrinkled leaves of a vegetable grown in Kashmir. Similar greens are also found in shops stocking vegetables for Chinese cooking. Large leaves of spinach can be substituted, but will have to be boiled for a minute in a little water and strained before use, taking care not to crush the leaves).
5 tbsp. mustard oil
½ tsp. asafoetida-water
1 tsp. salt, a pinch of baking soda
4 large green chilies, de-seeded and each broken into two
¼ tsp. spice cake (vari masala)

Preparation

Wash the hak thoroughly. Drain. Heat the oil. When smoking furiously, cover with a lid, leaving a little gap away from your side from where you should pour in the asafoetida water and 4 cups water. Remove the lid as soon as the loud sizzling stops. Add salt and chilies. When the oily water boils put in the hak leaves. Stir, turning the leaves well, so that all the sides are coated with an oily film. Cook, uncovered, on maximum heat, till the stalks are tender to the touch. Add the crushed spice cake (veri masala) before removing from heat. Serve hot. The gravy should resemble a very pale clear soup.

Dum Monji

(Browned Knol Khol/Kohlrabi)

Ingredients (Serves 8)

1 kg kohlrabi. Remove the leaves, peel and slice into 1 cm thick rounds.
1 cup oil
2 tsp. dry red chili powder
1½ tsp. dry ginger powder
2 tsp. fennel powder
5 cloves
1 black cardamom
2 tsp. salt
I tsp. garam masala

Preparation

Heat oil. Deep fry the kohlrabi slices in batches till a rich dark brown in color, taking care that they do not burn. The rest of the procedure is the same as for Dum Aloo (Browned Potatoes), except that it should have more gravy and that no ghee is used.

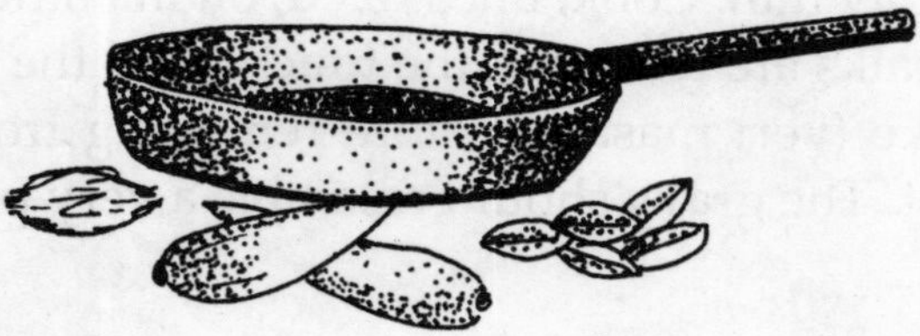

ALA ROGHANJOSH
(Pumpkin a la Roghanjosh)

Ingredients (Serves 8)

1 kg pumpkin. Peel and cut into large cubes 5 cm × 5 cm × 5 cm.

Preparation

Cook exactly as Dum Monji.

TSOK WANGUN
(Eggplant with Tamarind)

Ingredients (Serves 8 to 10)

1 cup oil (or enough to deep fry the eggplant pieces in batches)

2 pounds large eggplants. Wash, scrape off the thorny base and quarter lengthwise. If the eggplant is too thick, you may cut it into 6 or 8 lengths, but allow a bit of stem to remain with each segment.

3 tsp. chili powder

1½ tsp. dry ginger powder

2 tsp. fennel powder

5 cloves

¼ pound tamarind. Soak in a cup of water. Then strain through a sieve rubbing the pulp out.

4 green chilies. Cut into two.

Preparation

Heat oil. Deep fry the aubergines in small batches till brown, but not burnt. Strain and keep aside. Take 4 tbsp. of oil in a thick-bottomed vessel. While still hot, but removed from the heat, add the red chili powder with a tablespoon of water. Stir and add one cup of water. Put in the ginger and fennel powder, cloves and salt to taste. Add the fried aubergines. When boiling, add the cup of tamarind water and green chilies. Cook without a cover till half the water is absorbed. Finish off with ¼ tsp. of crushed black cumin seed. The aubergines should be tender, but not mushy.

Monji Kaliya
(Kohlrabi in Golden Gravy)

Ingredients (Serves 8)

2 pounds kohlrabi. Discard the leaves, peel and cut into 2 cm cubes.

Preparation

Deep fry the cubes till golden in color. Drain. Now cook exactly as Kaliya, the mutton disk in Kashmiri Pandit cuisine.

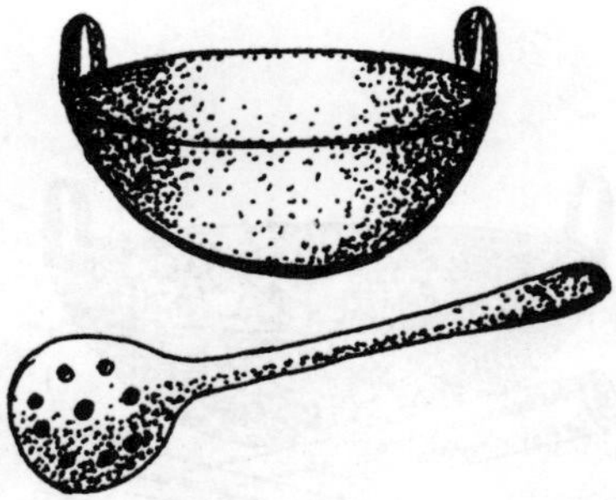

NADUR YAKHNI
(Lotus Root in Yoghurt Gravy)

Ingredients (Serves 8 to 10)

3 long, thick lotus roots (each about 40 cm long)

Preparation

Scrape the lotus stem clean, with a scraping knife. Cut into 5 cm lengths. Wash thoroughly, clearing the holes with a tooth pick, under a running tap. The cooking procedure is the same as that of Ala Yakhni (Marrow in Yoghurt Gravy).

Note: The gravy can be thickened with a table spoon of cornstarch worked into a paste with cold water and added to it while cooking.

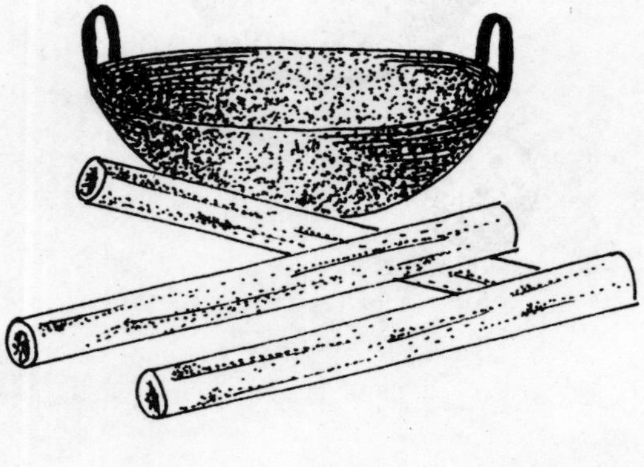

Nadur Palak

(Lotus Root with Spinach)

Ingredients (Serves 12)

5 tbsp. oil

½ pound lotus root. Scrape well and cut into ½ cm thick rounds. Wash thoroughly.

¼ tsp. asafoetida water

1 tsp. salt

2 pounds spinach. Clean, wash and chop coarsely.

1 tsp. dry red chili powder

½ tsp. turmeric

1 tsp. dry ginger powder

½ tsp. vari masala (spice-cake)

Preparation

Heat oil. Stir fry the lotus stem for 5 minutes, add asafoetida water, salt and the spinach. Stir-fry well till all the moisture is absorbed. Add the red chili powder, turmeric and ginger powder. Add 1 cup of water and cover with a lid. Simmer till the water is almost dry. Sprinkle the crushed vari masala and remove from heat.

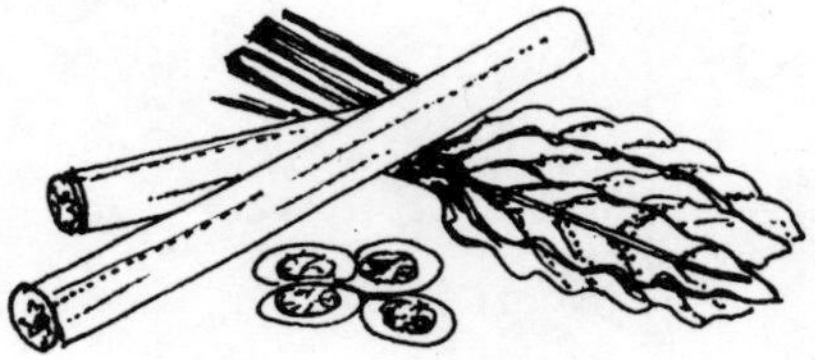

TAMATER WANGUN

(Tomato Eggplant Curry)

Ingredients (Serves 10)

½ cup oil
2 pounds eggplant. Wash; scrape clean the base and stems.
1 pound large tomatoes. Wash and quarter.
2 tsp. dry red chili powder
1 tsp. dry ginger powder
1½ tsp. turmeric powder
1½ tsp. salt
4 green chilies, broken into two

Preparation

Heat oil. Deep fry the eggplant in batches till light brown. Drain and keep aside. Heat 4 tbsp. of oil in a vessel or wok. Stir fry the quartered tomatoes, taking care that they do not break. Add the red chili, ginger, and turmeric powder. Stir and add 1 cup of water and salt. When it boils, put in the fried aubergines and halved green chilies. Cook till the water is reduced to half. Sprinkle a little powdered white cumin seed. Remove from heat and serve, either hot or cold.

Ala Yakhni
(Marrow in Yoghurt)

Ingredients (Serves 8)

¾ cup oil
2 cups marrow. Peel and cut into thick chunks (about 3 cm cubes)
3 tsp. fennel powder
1½ tsp. ginger powder
4 cloves
1 black cardamom
¼ tsp. asafoetida water
¼ tsp. cumin seed
16 ounces yoghurt. Whisk well
1 tbsp. ghee
3 green cardamoms (crushed)
½ tsp. garam masala powder

Preparation

Heat oil in a deep frying pan or wok. Deep fry the marrow chunks. Remove with a slotted spoon. Drain and keep aside. The marrow should not be allowed to brown.

Boil 1 cup water in a thick-bottomed vessel. Add salt, fennel and ginger powders, cloves, black cardamom, the asafoetida water and cumin. Add the marrow chunks. Pour the whisked yoghurt in, stirring all the time till smooth. Simmer till the gravy thickens to pouring custard consistency.

Contd. ...

Heat 3 tbsp. oil and 1 tbsp. ghee. Pour sizzling hot over the marrow. Add the crushed green cardamoms and garam masala. Remove from heat and serve hot.

Thsata Gogji
(Turnips in Clear Gravy)

Ingredients (Serves 8)

2 pounds turnips
4½ tbsp. mustard oil
1 tsp. salt
3 or 4 large red chilies
1 tsp. asafoetida water
3 cups water
¼ tsp vari masala (Kashmiri spice-cake)

Preparation

For this dish the turnips must not be peeled. They should be washed thoroughly after the top and the roots are cut off. Taking the turnip firmly in the left hand, shavings like thin wedges, about ½ cm on the thick side should then be taken off from all around it with a sharp knife. The cooking procedure is the same as for kohlrabi.

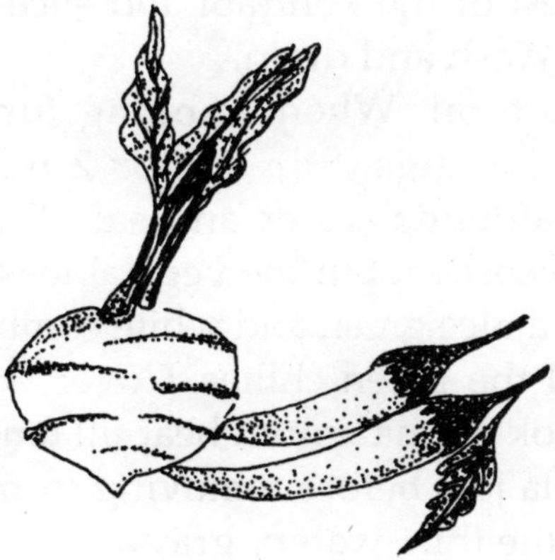

MONJIHAK
(Green and White Kohlrabi)

Ingredients (Serves 6-8)

2 pounds kohlrabi
6 tbsp. mustard oil
1 tsp. asafoetida water
1 tsp. salt
3 or 4 large red and green chilies, de-seeded and broken into two
3 cups water
¼ tsp. vari masala (spice cake)

Preparation

Discard all the discolored or unattractive looking leaves. Break each large leaf into two. Using a sharp knife, slice off the top including the small leaves from each kohlrabi. Cut this slice into two, discarding the little dense foliage in the center, as it is rather bitter. Peel the rest of the kohlrabi and slice into ½ cm thick shavings. Wash and drain.

Heat the oil. When smoking furiously, add the kohlrabi shavings. Stir fry for 2 minutes. Add the leaves, asafoetida water and salt. Stir fry till all the water is absorbed, but the vegetable is not browned. It should be a nice green and white combination. Add the water and the green chilies. Cover with a tightfitting lid and cook on maximum heat till tender. Sprinkle the vari masala just before removing from the heat. Serve hot, with the thin, watery gravy.

Razmah Gogji

(Kidney Beans with Turnips)

Ingredients (Serves 12-16)

3 cups kidney beans. (Clean and soak in 6 cups water overnight).
½ tsp. turmeric powder
Salt to taste
5 tbsp. oil
2 pounds turnip, peeled and quartered with edges smoothed as for Gogji Shabdegh (see page 73).
4 cloves garlic
½ tsp. black cumin seed
2-inch stick cinnamon
1 tsp. red chili powder
2 tsp. ginger powder
2 tsp. fennel powder
1 tbsp. asafoetida water
6 whole dry red chilies, de-seeded

Preparation

Discard the water in which the beans had been soaked. (It is best to use a pressure cooker for this dish). Boil 8 cups of water and the beans in an open pressure cooker. Add the turmeric powder and salt. Close the lid. Bring to high pressure, reduce heat and cook for 20 minutes, till the beans are soft, but not broken. A good test is to press a bean between the thumb and the index finger. If it bursts out of its skin in a floury mash,

Contd. ...

it is done. While the beans are cooking, heat oil in a deep frying pan. Add the turnips in batches, turning around frequently till very light brown in color. Drain and put into the beans. Meanwhile, remove the pan from the heat. While the oil is still hot, add the garlic, cumin seed, cinnamon, chili powder, ginger and fennel powder and 1 tbsp. water and then quickly pour over the beans and turnips in the pressure cooker. Add asafoetida water and red chilies. Close the lid, bring to pressure on high heat. Reduce heat and simmer for 5 minutes. Remove from heat and allow the pressure cooker to cool down to room temperature. Serve hot with rice.

Note: This dish can also be made with moong (whole green pulses) instead of rajmah (kidney beans). Moong will need only 10 minutes' pressure cooking. Another variation is moong (whole green pulse) with large cubes of peeled kohlrabi.

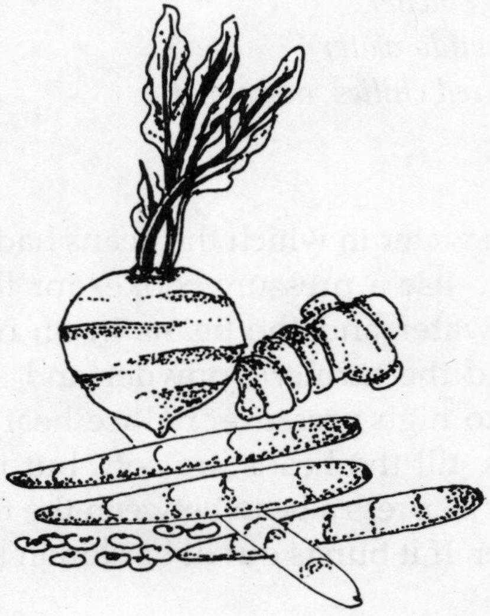

Shufta

Mitha Batta

Spices: Clockwise from top (outer circle): Red Chilly Powder, Salt, Black Cardamom, Cinnamon, Fennel Powder, Turmeric Powder, Ginger Powder and Spice Cake. (Inner circle): Green Cardamom, Asafoetida, Saffron and Cloves.

Monji Hak

TALITH MUJI CHATINEY
(Fried Grated Radish)

Ingredients (Serves 6-8)

2 pounds white radish
3 tbsp. mustard oil
1½ tsp. salt
1½ tsp. red chili powder
8 walnuts, chopped coarsely
½ tsp. black cumin seed

Preparation

Grate the radish finely. Heat the oil in a large kadahi (deep frying pan). When smoking for three minutes, add the radish. Stir-fry, till the water is completely absorbed. Add the salt, chili powder, chopped walnuts and cumin seed, while continuing to stir. Add 1 tbsp. water. Cover with a lid and simmer on low heat for 5 minutes. Remove lid, stir-fry till all the water is absorbed and the radish is evenly pink in color. Serve hot.

Bumtsoonth Nadur
(Quince with Lotus Stem)

Ingredients (Serves 8-10)

6 large quince
1 lb. lotus stem
¾ cup oil
3 cloves
1 tsp. turmeric powder
2 tsp. chili powder
1 tsp. yoghurt
1 stick cinnanmon
2 black cardamoms
½ level tsp. cumin powder
2 tsp. ginger powder
3 tsp. fennel powder
4 green chilies, each broken into two
1½ tsp. salt

Preparation

Peel, core and quarter the quince (cut each into 4 pieces). Scrape the lotus stem clean, wash and cut into ½-inch slices, diagonally.

Heat oil till it smokes. Fry the quince and lotus stem in batches till golden brown. Remove with a slotted spoon and keep aside. Take a thick-bottomed vessel. Heat 3 tbsp. oil and add the cloves. When they begin to sputter, remove the vessel from the heat and allow

Contd. ...

to cool slightly. Add the turmeric, chili powder and yoghurt. Stir well and heat again, adding the cinnamon, cardamoms and cumin. Add the fried quince and lotus stem, turning till the pieces are coated with the dark brown oil. Add a cup of water. When boiling, add the ginger, fennel powder and green chilies. Season with salt. Close with a tight-fitting lid and simmer on gentle heat till the water is absorbed. Serve hot.

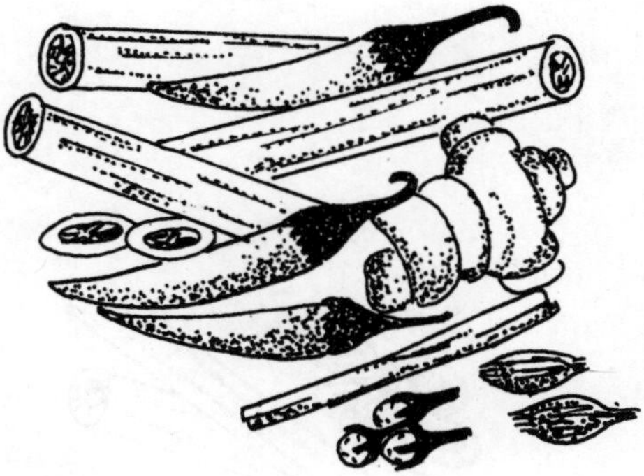

Bumtsoonth Wangun
(Quince with Aubergine)

Ingredients (Serves 8-10)

The same as for Bumsoonth Nadur (Quince with Lotus stem), substituting 2 pounds eggplant for lotus stem.

Preparation

Follow the same process as for Quince with Lotus Stem. Cut eggplant lengthwise into four.

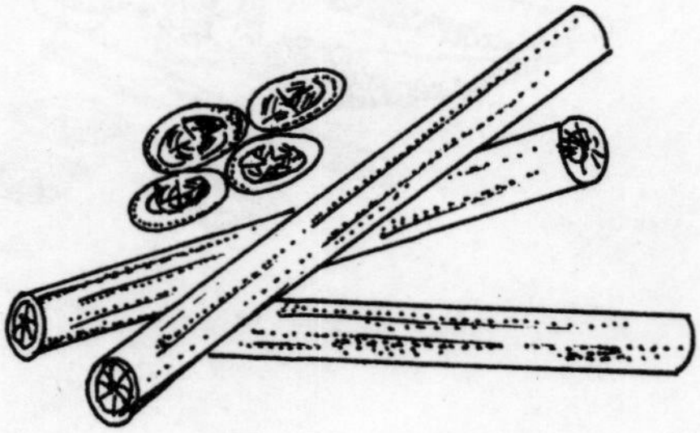

Tsoonth Wangun

(Apples with Aubergine)

Follow the procedure as for Quince with Lotus Stem, using any sourish variety of apples and eggplants (see page 57).

Ingredients (Serves 8-10)

The same as for Bumtsoonth Nadur (Quince with Lotus Stem), substituting 6 large apples (any sour variety) for quince and 2 pounds eggplant for lotus stem.

Preparation

Follow the same procedure as for Quince with Lotus Stem. Cut eggplant lengthwise into four.

Morels

Morels are a type of edible fungi which grow wild in the forests at high elevations in the state of Jammu and Kashmir. Unlike mushrooms, morels cannot be artificially cultivated and this makes them very expensive, and highly prized. Fresh morels, a rare delicacy, are available only in spring when they are in season. It is then that they are gathered and dried for use.

KANAGUCHHI

(Morels in Yoghurt Sauce)

Ingredients (Serves 8)

3 tbsp. oil or ghee
1 onion. Slice finely.
5 cloves garlic. Peel and crush.
½ cup dried morels. Soak in hot water for one hour and then wash thoroughly, rinsing several times so that they are not gritty. Squeeze out the water and keep aside.
Salt to taste
1 cup yoghurt. Whisk well.
1 tsp. ginger powder
2 tsp. fennel powder

½ tsp. cumin, crushed
1 tsp. garam masala

Preparation

Heat oil or ghee in a saucepan. Add the onions and stir-fry for two minutes. Do not allow them to brown. Put in the garlic and, after a minute, the morels and salt. Toss around the pan till all the water is evaporated. Add one cup of water. When boiling, pour in the whisked yoghurt. Put in the ginger and fennel powders and keep stirring so that the gravy does not curdle. When boiling and smooth, reduce heat and allow to simmer till the gravy is the consistency of thin custard. Sprinkle the crushed cumin and garam masala on top. Remove from heat after two minutes. Serve hot.

MITHA KANAGUCHHI

(Morels in Syrup)

Ingredients (Serves 8)

½ cup dried morels. Clean and prepare as in the previous recipe.
3 tablespoons ghee
1 cup sugar
4 cups water
6 green cardamoms
¼ tsp. saffron. Crush with a little warm water.
2 tsp. lemon juice

Preparation

Lightly fry the morels in the ghee. Drain and keep aside. Dissolve the sugar in water over low heat. Once dissolved, bring to boil and add the morels, cardamom and saffron. Cook till the morels become nicely swollen and the syrup is thickened. Add the lemon juice and serve hot or cold.

Hedar
(Mushrooms)

Ingredients (Serves 4)

¾ cup button mushrooms
3 tablespoons ghee
1 small onion. Slice finely.
2 cloves garlic. Clean and crush.
½ tsp. salt
½ tsp. red chili powder
a pinch of black pepper powder
1 tsp. flour
1 cup milk
½ cup water

Preparation

Wash and quarter the mushrooms, slicing off a thin strip from the base.

Heat the ghee in a saucepan. Add the onions and garlic and stir-fry for two minutes. Add the mushrooms and salt. Stir well. Cover and simmer till the moisture is absorbed. Put in the chili and pepper powder and flour, stirring well. Add the milk and water and simmer till the gravy is thick. Serve hot.

Dried Vegetables

Some vegetables are dried in the dry autumn of Kashmir. One of the most colorful sights in Kashmir in autumn are the garlands of deep red chilies strung like coral, the cream of white marrow slices strung on thread and green hak, like some large exotic beads, that hang from eaves, windows and balconies to dry in the gentle warmth of the sun. Apples too are sliced and dried in the same way to be cooked as a vegetable in winter. Bunches of mint and other herbs, tucked into alcoves to dry, add to the colorful scene.

Once dehydrated, they keep well and are readily available in the winter months when they are no longer in season. Turnips, along with their long leaves, are prepared thus for drying: pick firm, leafy turnips. Clean and dip in boiling, salted water for one minute. Drain and pat dry. Using a sharp knife, cut off the root and, from the root side, divide each turnip into four lengthwise, without cutting through, so that a little bit on top remains undivided, and the quarters are held together by the leaves. Hang the turnip from a nail or hook and plait the leaves together. Leave the long plaits hanging in a sunny place till quite dry. Store for use only when there is no sign of moisture or dampness.

Marrows, tomatoes and eggplants are the other vegetables commonly dried. The marrow is peeled before dipping it in boiling water. Tomatoes are sliced, eggplants quartered lengthwise and marrow cut into 2 cm thick slices for drying.

GOGJIPUNI
(Dried Turnips with Leaves)

Ingredients (Serves 8)

1 pound dried turnips with leaves
6 cups water, divided
4 tbsp. oil
½ tsp. asafoetida water or 6 cloves garlic crushed
1 tsp. salt
3 large red or green chilies
¼ tsp. vari masala (spice cake)

Preparation

Unravel the leaves and break roughly without tearing the turnips. Put into a pan. Bring 3 cups of water to a boil. Pour over the turnips in the pan and let them soak for half an hour. Drain, pressing the water out. Wash and drain again. Heat oil in a vessel. When smoking, stir in the crushed garlic and put in the drained vegetables and stir fry for five minutes. Add the salt and 3 cups water. Put in the chilies, each broken into two. Cook till soft. About 2 cups of water should remain and it should be pale cream in color. Sprinkle the crushed vari masala over the preparation, and remove from heat. Serve hot.

ALA HUCHI WANGAN
(Dried Marrow with Aubergine)

Ingredients (Serves 6-8)

4½ cups water, divided
½ lb. dried eggplant quarters
½ lb. dried marrow slices
5 tbsp. oil
1 tsp. cumin
1 tbsp. yoghurt
2 tsp. chili powder
1 tsp. turmeric powder
1 tsp. powdered ginger
2 tsp. fennel powder
1 tsp. salt
½ tsp. vari masala (spice cake)

Preparation

Boil 3 cups water. Pour over the dried vegetables in a pan. Soak for half an hour. Drain the vegetables, throwing away the water. Heat oil in a pan. When smoking, stir in the cumin, yoghurt, chili and turmeric powder. After 2 minutes, add 1½ cups water. When boiling, put in the ginger and fennel powder and the drained vegetables. Cook till soft. Add salt. The gravy should be a rich brown in color. Sprinkle the crushed vari masala on top. This is a rather spicy curry and can be enjoyed with plain rice and yoghurt.

Everyday Non-Vegetarian Food

Kashmiris are voracious meat-eaters, mutton being their main preference. A meal served without at least one mutton dish is considered to be not only incomplete, but almost a deprivation! The very idea of offering a meatless meal to a guest is a not-to-be-suffered embarrassment. There is thus a great variety of mutton dishes in Kashmiri cuisine, some of which use all kinds of vegetables too. A standard Kashmiri meal with its servings of rice, mutton, leafy and other vegetables, chutney or mint, walnut or radish, depending upon the season, and yoghurt is therefore quite a balanced one. Fish is also a very important part of the menu, particularly in winter. The rivers and lakes are full of fresh-water fish, mostly of the carp family. Trout is found in mountain streams and fishing is a popular sport. Mahseer is also found at some places.

EVERYDAY MUTTON DISHES

Palak Maaz

(Mutton with Spinach)

Ingredients (Serves 8)

8 tbsp. oil
2 pounds mutton, cut into medium-sized pieces. A mixture of lean and fatty mutton is best.
2 pounds spinach. Wash thoroughly, remove stalks keeping the leaves whole.
¼ tsp. asafoetida water
1 tsp. salt
4 cloves
2 tsp. red chili powder
2 tsp. ginger powder
½ tsp. vari masala (spice cake)

Preparation

Heat oil. Stir-fry the mutton for a few minutes to seal in the juices. Add the spinach leaves and asafoetida water, salt and cloves. Stir well. Cook till the spinach water is absorbed, stirring occasionally. Add the chili and ginger powder and some water if the mutton is still tough. Cover with a tight-fitting lid and cook till tender. Sprinkle the crushed spice cake before removing from heat.

MATAR KEEMA
(Mince with Peas)

Ingredients (Serves 8 to 10)

2 cups water
2 pounds minced meat
8 tbsp. oil
3 cloves
3 black cardamoms
2 medium-sized onions, chopped fine
2 cloves of garlic, crushed
1 tsp. ginger powder
1 inch piece ginger, chopped fine
4 medium-sized tomatoes, chopped fine or puréed
2 pounds green peas
1 tsp. salt
1 tsp. red chili powder
1 medium stick cinnamon
2 tsp. fennel powder

Preparation

Boil the water. Add the mince, stirring well so that it is finely mixed with the water. Cook till the mince is soft and most of the water absorbed.

Heat the oil. Add the cloves, crushed cardamom, cumin and onions. Stir-fry till the onions are golden brown. Add the garlic and ginger. Stir-fry for 2 minutes. Add the puréed tomatoes. Stir-fry for 5 minutes. Put

Contd. ...

in the peas and salt. Stir-fry for another 2 minutes. Add the chili, cinnamon and fennel powder. Stir well. Now add the mince with the remaining water. Cover with a tight-fitting lid and cook on medium heat till the peas are soft and the liquid almost dry. Sprinkle the garam masala powder, just before removing from the heat.

You may garnish with chopped green coriander and a few halved green chilies.

Clockwise from left: Tsamun, Hak, Nadur

Dum Kokur and Plain Rice

Kehwa being poured out of a Samawar

Aab Gosh

METHIMUTHS
(Fenugreek and Minced Meat)

Ingredients (Serves 12 to 16)

2 pounds minced meat, finely minced
2 pounds fenugreek leaves, washed, cleaned and chopped roughly
8 tbsp. oil
1 tbsp. red chili powder
1 tbsp. ginger powder
2 tsp. fennel powder
½ tsp. turmeric
3 cloves
½ tsp. black cumin

Preparation

Prepare the minced meat as for koftas (page 30), using the same quantity of spices. Knead well. Form into small balls the size of marbles (50 to 60).

Boil 2 cups of water in a pan. When boiling, add the minced meat balls. Cook till the balls are spongy (they should feel firm outside). The gravy should be reduced to about half-a-cup by the time this stage of the cooking is reached.

Heat oil in a thick-bottomed pan. Put the cloves in. Add the washed fenugreek leaves. Stir-fry till almost dry. Now add the turmeric, chili and ginger powder. Stir well. Pour the stock with the minced meat balls in. Cover with a lid. Cook till all the water is absorbed. Serve hot.

Gogji Shabdegh
(Mutton with Turnips)

Ingredients (Serves 8)

6 tbsp. oil
3-4 cloves
2 pounds mutton. Fatty mutton is a must for this dish. Cut into medium-sized pieces.
2 pounds turnips. Clean and peel medium-sized turnips and cut each turnip into quarters. Smoothen the cut edges by knifing off the sharp corners and peeling a thin shaving from the edges.
1½ tsp. salt
1 tsp. asafoetida water
3 black cardamoms, coarsely ground
½ tsp. chili powder
4 cups water
2 tsp. turmeric powder
3 tsp. fennel powder
2 tsp. ginger powder
1 tsp. garam masala
½ tsp. Kashmiri spice-cake

Preparation

Heat oil in a thick-bottomed vessel. Add the cloves and immediately afterwards, the mutton. Stir and cover with a lid for 5 minutes. Turn over the pieces of mutton so that all the juices are sealed in. After 5 minutes add the turnips and salt and asafoetida water and cardamom. Cook and turn over frequently so that the turnips too are lightly browned on all sides. Stir in the chili powder. Add the water and, when boiling, put in turmeric, fennel and ginger powder together, stirring well but taking care not to break or crush the turnips. Cover with a tight-fitting lid and simmer over gentle heat till the meat is tender and the turnips very soft to the touch, but not crushed. Just before removing from heat, sprinkle the garam masala and crushed spice cake over, cover and then serve hot. All the water should not have dried up, because an essential feature of this dish is its gravy.

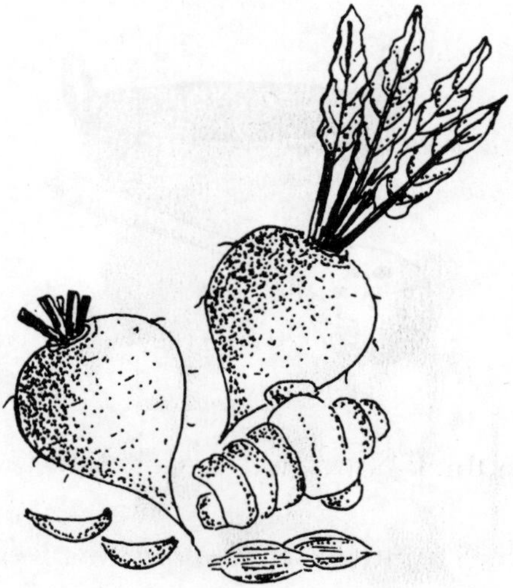

Monjimaaz
(Mutton with Kohlrabi)

Ingredients (Serves 8)

The same as for Gogji Shabdegh, substituting 2 pounds kohlrabi for the turnips. Peel and cut like the turnips in Gogji Shabdegh.

Preparation

Cook exactly like Gogji Shabdegh.

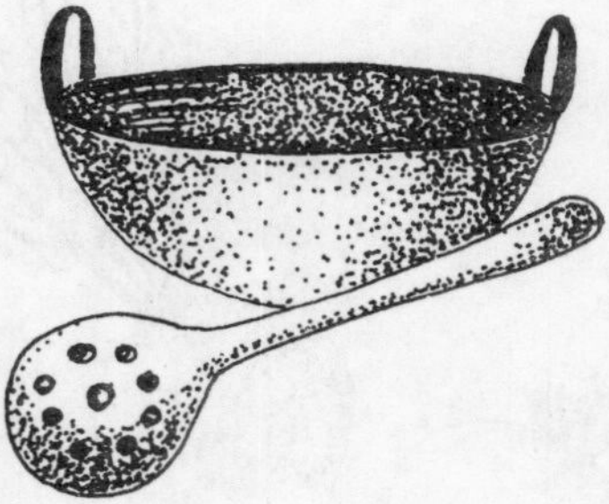

ALU MAAZ
(Mutton with Potatoes)

Ingredients (Serves 8)

The same as for Gogji Shabdegh substituting 2 pounds medium-sized potatoes for the turnips. Peel and cut into halves.

Preparation

Cook exactly like Gogji Shabdegh.

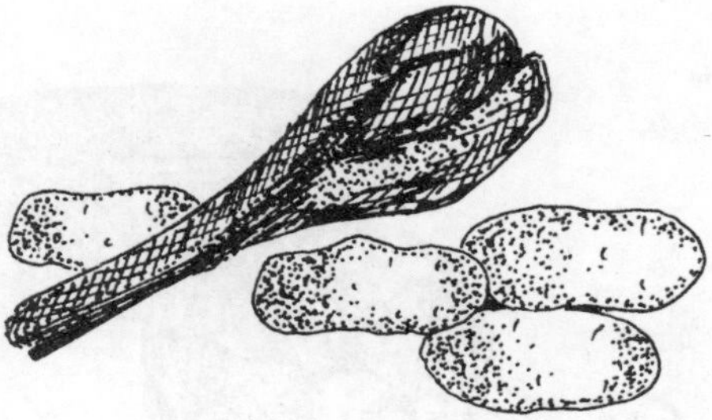

BUND GOOBI MAAZ
(Mutton with Cabbage)

Ingredients (Serves 8)

The same as for Gogji Shabdegh substituting 2 pounds cabbage for the turnips

Preparation

The procedure is the same as for Gogji Shabdegh. The cabbage is cut into large chunks.

TSOK TSARVAN
(Liver in Tamarind Sauce)

Ingredients (Serves 12 to 20)

4 tbsp. oil
¼ pound onion, slice finely
5 cloves of garlic. Skin, and crush.
2 pounds liver, cleaned and cut into 1-inch cubes
1 tsp. salt
2 tsp. red chili powder
1½ tsp. dry ginger powder
2 tsp. fennel powder
¼ pound tamarind. Soak in a little warm water for half an hour. Rub through a fine sieve and make into a cupful with water.
¼ tsp. sugar
1 tsp. garam masala

Preparation

Heat oil in a thick-bottomed pan. Add the onions. Stir-fry till transparent, not browned. Add the garlic. Cover and cook for one minute. Add the liver cubes and salt. Stir well and fry for 10 minutes. Add 2 tbsp. water and chili powder. Stir till the color turns a dark brown. Add the ginger and fennel powder. Stir well. Pour in the tamarind water. Add sugar. Cook till half the water is absorbed and the oil begins to separate. Sprinkle the garam masala. Cook for another 2 minutes. Serve hot. Makes an excellent breakfast dish.

Fish and Fowl Dishes

Kashmiris are very fond of fish, though it cannot take the place of mutton in their cuisine. Though it is widely eaten in winter and spring, no fish dishes form part of the 'wazawan'. The Pandits must have it at Shivaratri, a festival that, among other things, marks the end of winter. One of the most popular winter-time delicacies sold at roadside stalls is 'phari', whole fish, batter-coated and smoked.

Lakes and swamps attract a large variety of wild duck. Duck shooting is a popular sport in the open season. It is interesting to note that orthodox Kashmiri Pandits, who would not touch chicken or eggs as 'unclean', relish wild fowl and their eggs, thinking perhaps that inhabiting the airy spheres, these creatures cannot feed upon domestic rubbish!

PUCHHIN DUMPOKHTA
(Pot-roasted Spicy Wild Duck)

Ingredients (Serves 4)

½ cup oil
1 medium-sized onion, sliced finely
1 whole garlic pod. Peel and crush all the cloves.
One medium-sized wild duck. Pluck the feathers. Slit in front and clean the inside. Smoke on a charcoal fire so that all the bits of fluff are burnt away. Wash and clean well. Cut into medium-sized pieces.
5 cloves
3 black cardamoms, ground coarsely
1½ tsp. salt
2 tsp. red chili powder
¼ cup yoghurt
2 tsp. ginger powder
3 tsp. fennel powder
5 peppercorns
3 bay leaves
1 stick cinnamon
Some dough for sealing the lid
½ inch cube of vari masnla

Preparation

Heat oil in a thick-bottomed pan. When smoking, add the onions and stir-fry for two minutes. Put in the crushed garlic. Immediately after, add the wild duck along with cloves, cardamom and salt. Keep covered, but stir frequently till all the water is absorbed and all the pieces are browned well. Put in the chili powder and yoghurt and stir and turn till all the pieces are nicely coated with the oil-chili-yoghurt mixture. Add 1 cup of water. When boiling, put in the ginger and fennel powders, peppercorns and bay leaves. Add cinnamon stick. Cover and seal the lid with the dough. Reduce heat and allow to simmer for about an hour. Open the lid and sprinkle crushed vari masala. All the water should have been absorbed by this time. Serve hot with rice.

Lotus stem, scraped clean and cut into 4 cm lengths and halved lengthwise, can also be added to the wild fowl while it is cooking. It is believed that the 'hot' fowl and the 'cool' lotus stem make a healthy combination.

Gada

(Traditional Kashmiri Fish Curry)

Ingredients (Serves 6-8)

¾ cup mustard oil

2 pounds fish. Kashmiris use carp, but any fish variety good for curry can be used. Clean the fish thoroughly. Wash and cut into medium-sized pieces. Rub a little salt and turmeric on the pieces and keep aside.

2 tsp. tumeric powder

2 tsp. salt

2 tsp. ginger powder

3 tsp. fennel powder

5 cloves

6 peppercorns

4 cloves of garlic or asafoetida water

2 tsp. red chili powder

1 inch piece of vari masala

½ tsp. black cumin

Preparation

Heat oil in a kadahi or deep frying pan. When sizzling hot, fry the fish in batches of three or four pieces till brown in color. When all the pieces are done, take 4 cups of water in a thick-bottomed pan and gently lower the still warm, fried fish into it. Add the turmeric, salt, ginger and fennel powders, cloves, peppercorns, crushed garlic or asafoetida water. Place the red chili powder in a neat little heap on top and quickly pour

6 tbsp. of hot oil on it. Cook on high heat till the gravy is thick and the fish soft, but the pieces should not be broken. A couple of minutes before removing from the heat, sprinkle the crushed vari and cumin.

This is the basic recipe but it can be varied in a number of ways, all quite popular items of Kashmiri cuisine. Some of these other fish dishes, using the traditional fish curry as a base, are as follows.

Muji Gada

(Fish with Radish)

Cut 1 pound large white radish into 1 cm wide slices. Wash well, drain and pat dry. Deep fry to a light brown color. Drain with a slotted spoon and put into the fish curry while it is cooking.

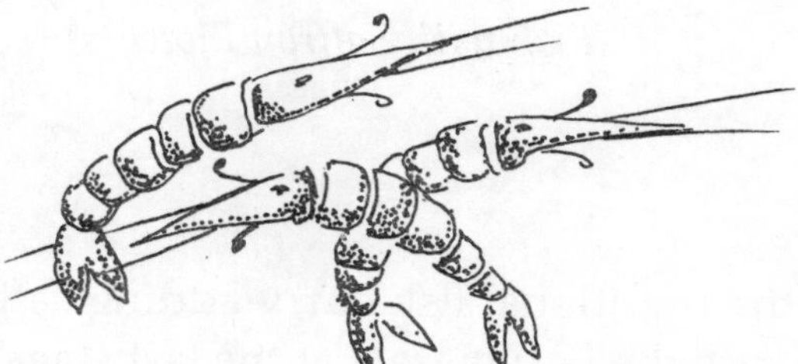

Monji Gada
(Fish with Kohlrabi)

Peel 2 pounds kohlrabi and cut into 1 cm thick slices. Use like the radish in the recipe for Muji Gada.

Gada Nadur
(Fish with Lotus Stem)

Scrape two long lotus stems (about 2 feet long) clean. Cut into 4 cm lengths, halving them lengthwise. Wash well. Fry lightly and add to the fish curry like the radish in the recipe for Muji Gada.

Kong Gada
(Fish with Saffron Flowers)

Cook the traditional fish curry adding saffron flowers along with the vari masala at the last stage of cooking.

HOGADA
(Dried Fish)

Ingredients (Serves 8)

1 pound dried fish of any kind
4 tbsp. mustard oil
½ tsp. asafoetida water or 4 cloves garlic
1½ tbsp. red chili powder
1 tsp. turmeric powder
3 cups water
1 tsp. ginger powder
1 tsp. fennel powder
1 tsp. salt
½ tsp. vari masala. (spice-cake)

Preparation

Scrape the fish clean, removing the blackened film of skin, if any. Wash and pat dry. If the fish is too large, cut into medium-sized pieces. Heat oil in a pan. Before it starts smoking, put in the fish. Stir-fry till it has been sizzling for about five minutes. Add the asafoetida water or crushed garlic, chili and turmeric powder, and 3 cups of water. When boiling, put in the ginger and fennel powder. Add salt. Simmer till the fish is done. It should not be too soft. Kashmiris like their hogada to be chewable and slightly crunchy. Crumble vari masala over top before serving.

HOGADA HAK

(Dried Fish with Greens)

Ingredients (Serves 8)

Same as for Hagada
½ pound hak leaves

Preparation

This dish is prepared in the same way as Hogada. The hak leaves are put in when the fish is being fried and then cooked along with it.

HOGADA BOOM

(Dried Fish with Water Lily Roots)

Ingredients (Serves 8)

Same as for Hogada
A bunch of *dried wafer lily roots*

Preparation

The long roots of the water lilies are broken and soaked in hot water for half an hour. They are then drained and put in when the fish is being fried and cooked along with it.

Sheer Chai

Left to right: Nadur Monji, Nadur Cnurma, Muji Chatini

Vegetarian Thal (A Typical Kashmiri Pandit Festive Meal)

Hak

PHARI
(Batter-coated Smoked Fish)

Ingredients (Serves 8)

8 tsp. rice floor
2 tsp. red chili powder
½ tsp. turmeric powder
¼ tsp. salt
8 cloves of garlic, ground to a paste
½ tsp. black cumin
8 medium-sized well-dried fish
2 tbsp. oil

Preparation

Make a thick batter with the rice flour and all the spices. Keep aside. Clean the fish thoroughly, scraping off the skin. Wash and pat dry. Soak the fish in the batter for 15 mins. Put the oil in a shallow, thick-bottomed pan. When smoking, add the fish and smoke till golden-brown and crisp. (A winter delicacy.)

Rice

Rice is the staple food of the Kashmiris. They eat it plain boiled with accompanying meat and vegetable dishes. Festive food, however, includes special rice dishes, which are given in this chapter.

Pulao

(Saffron Mutton Rice)

Ingredients (Serves 10-12)

8 tbsp. ghee
1 large onion. Slice finely.
5 cloves of garlic. Peel and crush.
1 inch cube of ginger. Grate finely.
2 pounds mutton, boneless, cut into 2-inch pieces
2 black cardamoms. Grind coarsely.
5 green cardamoms. Crush.
3 cloves
4 bay leaves
1 inch stick cinnamon
6 black peppercorns
¼ tsp. sugar
2 tsp. salt
¼ tsp. saffron. Soak in a little warm milk.
2 pounds rice long grained basmati rice. Clean, wash and soak in water for an hour.
1 cup yoghurt. Whisk well.
2 cups of wholemeal flour. Knead with a little water to form a ball of dough.
4 tbsp. blanched, halved almonds. Fry lightly.

Preparation

Heat the ghee in a thick-bottomed pan. When smoking, put in the onions and stir fry till transparent. Do not allow them to brown. Add the crushed garlic and ginger. Stir fry for two minutes. Put in the mutton. Turn the pieces around for a while. Cover and cook for 5 minutes. Add all the spices and yoghurt. Simmer till the meat is tender. You may need to add a little water while it is cooking, but at the end there should not remain more than half a cup of gravy.

Boil the rice in about 12 cups of water in a large pan. When the rice is half done, drain off the water till the grains of rice feel quite dry. Test by crushing a grain between the thumb and index finger. It should feel soft outside, but have a slightly hard core. Gently turn the rice out into a large basin and pour the mutton and its gravy over it. Mix it all together with a light, gentle touch so that the grains of rice do not break or the mutton pieces disintegrate. Transfer the mixture back into the large pan and cover with a tight-fitting lid. Seal with the dough, stretching it all around the pan so that the steam cannot escape. Cook on low heat for 15 minutes. When uncovered, the rice should look fluffy and stretched to its full length. Garnish with the almonds and serve hot.

BUZBHATTA
(Vegetable Pulao)

Ingredients (Serves 4-6)

5 tbsp. ghee
2 cloves
1 tsp. white cumin
1 onion, sliced fine
2 black cardamoms
1 stick cinnamon
2 bay leaves
1 cup cauliflower. Cut into florets
1 cup potato, peeled and cut into cubes
1 cup shelled green peas
½ cup carrot, scraped and cut into neat cubes
2 cups rice. Wash and drain
1 tsp. ginger powder
¼ tsp. turmeric powder
½ tsp. sugar
1 tsp. black cumin

Preparation

Heat ghee in a thick-bottomed vessel. When it smokes, put in the cloves and white cumin and let them sizzle for a few seconds. Stir-fry the onions till they become translucent. Now add the crushed black cardamom, cinnamon, bay leaves and immediately after, the vegetables. Stir-fry and cook with a lid on for 5 minutes to seal in the juices. Stir in the rice, mixing all the ingredients together. Add 4 cups of water, ginger and turmeric powders, sugar and black cumin. Cover with a tight-fitting lid and cook on medium heat till all the water is absorbed and the rice fluffy. Serve hot.

Mitha Bhatta/Zarda

(Sweet Saffron Rice)

Ingredients (Serves 4-6)

1 cup wholemeal flour dough
2 cups long grained basmati rice. Wash and soak
5 tbsp. ghee
3 tbsp. blanched and halved almonds
3 tbsp. Cashew nuts, halved
3 tbps. coconut. Cut into very thin (2 cm long) strips
3 tbsp. raisins. Wash and pat dry
1¾ cups sugar
½ tsp. saffron. Soak in a little warm milk.
8 green cardamoms, crushed

Preparation

Knead 1 cup of whole-meal flour to make dough for sealing. Keep aside till required. Boil the rice in plenty of water and drain when the rice is half done. Heat the ghee in a thick-bottomed vessel. Put in the almonds, cashew nuts, coconut strips and raisins. Stir fry for a minute. Add the drained half-done rice, sugar, saffron and crushed cardamoms. Stir, mixing all the ingredients well. Reduce heat. Cover with a lid, sealing it with dough all around. Allow to cook for 15 minutes on low heat. The rice should be fluffy and attractively lemon colored. Garnish with a few more fried cashew nuts.

VER

(Festive Spicy Rice Gruel)

Ver is made only on two special occasions in Kashmiri Pandit households : one is the betrothal of a son or daughter and the other is the eve of the wedding, just before henna is applied to the hands of the groom or bride. Kashmiris, as a rule, are not fond of sweets, hence it is not surprising that the special preparation on these two important occasions is not the sweet 'kheer', but the hot and spicy ver.

Ingredients (Serves 4-6)

¼ pound mutton fat or ½ cup walnuts
3 tbsp. mustard oil
1 cup good quality Kashmiri rice. Wash and soak in water for an hour
3 tsp. asafoetida water (1 gm asafoetida soaked in 3 tsp. water)
6 cups water
1 tsp. salt
½ tsp. cumin
1 tsp. crushed spice cake (the asafoetida flavored one)

Preparation

If using mutton fat, wash it well and break into small lumps. Lightly fry in a little oil and asafoetida water and keep aside. Heat oil in a large saucepan. When it

Contd. ...

smokes, put in the rice and asafoetida water. Stir-fry for a minute. Add 6 cups of water, salt and the mutton fat or walnuts. Cook till the rice is very soft and the consistency of thick gruel. Sprinkle the cumin and spice cake on top. Stir and serve hot.

Desserts

Sweets are not a very important item of Kashmiri cuisine. Hot, spicy food is what is most popular. There are, however, a few desserts that Kashmiri Muslims serve at the end of a marriage feast or as part of Id festivities. The Kashmiri Pandits also prepare sweet dishes on religious festivals, birthdays and for pujas.

Shufta
(Cottage Cheese in Syrup)

Ingredients (Serves 20 to 25)

2 cups sugar
2 tsp. lemon juice
8-10 tbsp. ghee
1 lb. (16 ounces) cottage cheese, cut into 1 cm cubes or the size of small raisins
½ lb. (8 oz) shelled almonds (small size). Blanch
½ lb. (8 oz) raisins or currants. Remove stalks, wash and pat dry
½ cup dates. Wash and cut into small pieces the size of raisins
¼ tsp. saffron. Soak in a little warm water.
15 green cardamoms, crushed
1 tbsp. poppy seeds. Clean, wash and pat dry

Preparation

Boil 3 cups of water. Add the sugar. Stir and simmer the syrup till smooth. Add the lemon juice and keep aside. Heat the ghee and fry the cheese cubes in batches till a light brown (not burnt) in color. Drain and toss into the cooled syrup. Fry all the nuts and dry fruit lightly. Drain and add to the syrup. Let the syrup boil again. Add the soaked and crushed saffron and cardamom. Sprinkle the poppy seeds on top and remove from the heat. It is a delicious dessert, and will especially appeal to those with a sweet tooth.

Gari Halwa
(Water-Chestnut Flour Dessert)

Ingredients (Serves 8)

2 cups water-chestnut flour, sieved
1 cup ghee (clarified butter)
1½ cups sugar
2 cups water
1 tsp. poppy seeds
A few almonds, blanched and halved
6 green cardamom seeds, crushed

Preparation

Heat a wok or thick-bottomed deep frying pan. Put in the flour and stir around on medium heat for a few minutes, till the flour turns a light brown and its aroma can be smelt. Add the ghee. Stir-fry till a rich brown in color. Put in the sugar and water together. Keep stirring till the water is absorbed and the mixture leaves the sides of the pan. Sprinkle the poppy seeds, almonds and cardamom and remove from the heat. Serve hot.

PHIRIN
(Rice Flour Dessert)

Ingredients (Serves 8)

2 tbsp. fine quality rice. Soak overnight
6 cups milk
4 tbsp. sugar
2 tbsp. blanched almonds, shredded
A few stamens of saffron. Soak in a little warmed milk.
A few drops of rose water
Silver leaf

Preparation

Grind the soaked rice to a fine paste. Add to the milk and bring to a boil. Put in the sugar and the almonds. Simmer for five minutes. Just before removing from heat, put in the soaked saffron and rose water. Ladle out into small earthenware bowls and chill before serving. Decorate with silver leaf.

Kofta Khumani
(Mince Apricots)

Ingredients (Serves 10—12)

2 pounds minced meat, minced very finely
2 black cardamoms, crushed
¼ tsp. white zeera
2 cloves
1 stick cinnamon
¼ lb. potato. Boil till soft
1 tsp. flour
1 egg
20 almonds, blanched and halved
2 cups sugar
A pinch of saffron
8 green cardamoms, crushed
1 lemon (juice)

Preparation

Boil ¾ cup water. Add the minced meat and spices and almonds. Cover the lid of the vessel and cook till the water is absorbed. Cool. Pound the spiced mince, boiled potatoes and 1 tsp. flour together. Add one egg and knead thoroughly. Wet your palms and form into small, flattened balls the size of apricots, with a halved, blanched almond tucked inside. Keep aside. (You should be able to make about 40 to 45 'apricots'.)

Contd. ...

Boil 2 cups of water with 2 cups of sugar till the syrup is slightly thinner than the consistency of honey. Add a pinch of saffron, crushed with a little water, and 8 ground green cardamoms. Gently lower the 'apricots' in the syrup. Cover with a lid. Cook for 10 minutes. Add 1 tsp. lemon juice and serve hot or cold, as preferred.

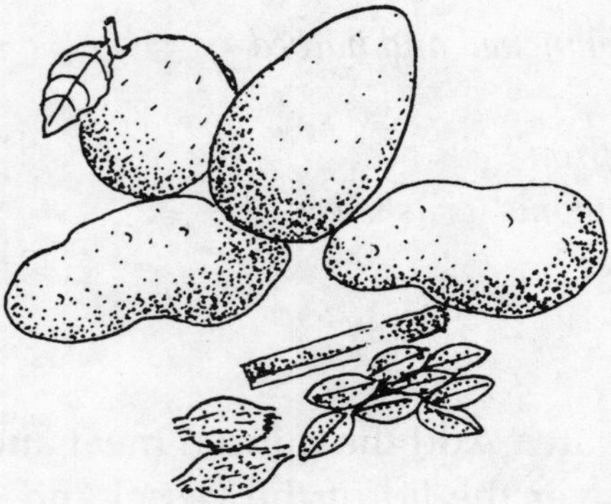

Beverages

Kashmiris are great tea drinkers. Their predilection for hot drinks is not surprising in view of the climate — temperature can plunge to minus 10 degrees celsius in winter. Tea is the favorite drink and many different kinds are used to make interesting brews. If the Ramadan occurs in summer, refreshing cool drinks are prepared to break the day-long fast. There is also a drink prepared with fermented (but non-alcoholic) rice water, which is also used to flavor some fish dishes.

Kahwa
(Green Tea)

Ingredients (Serves 8)

2 tsp. green tea
9 cups of water
8 stamens of saffron
8 green cardamoms, powdered
1 stick cinnamon, powdered
12 almonds, blanched and crushed or slivered into flakes
12 tsp. sugar (more or less to taste)

Preparation

Add the tea, crushed between your palms, to a vessel containing 9 cups of cold water and saffron. While waiting for the tea to boil, arrange 8 warmed cups and saucers on a tray. Divide the powdered cardamom, cinnamon and crushed almonds into eight portions and put in the cups.

As soon as the tea boils, add the sugar. Bring to a boil again and pour into the cups containing the powdered condiments, using a tea strainer to keep the leaves out. Serve steaming hot. Excellent on a cold day or for a cold in the head.

Sheer Chai
(Salt Tea with Cream or 'Malai')

Ingredients (Serves 8)

4 heaped tsp. of tea leaves (Pahar tea)
1 pinch baking soda
3 cups milk
½ tsp. salt
8 cardamoms, crushed
8 almonds, crushed
8 tsp. malai or cream

Preparation

Boil 1½ cups of water in a medium-sized saucepan. As soon as the water is boiling, add the tea leaves and the baking soda. Boil till the liquid is reduced to ¼ cup and its color is a dark maroon with 'dirty pink' froth. At this stage, put in 5 cups of water, 3 cups of milk and ½ tsp. salt. When it boils, the color should be a peachy pink.

Arrange 8 cups in a tray. Keep a spoonful of the cardamom-almond mixture aside. Divide the rest into 8 portions and put into each cup. Pour the boiling tea over. Top off with a level tsp. of malai or cream. Sprinkle a pinch of the almond-cardamom powder over and serve hot. This tea makes an interesting soup substitute. Let your guests guess the basic ingredients!

Babribyol Sherbet

(Sweet Basil Drink)

Ingredients (Serves 8)

2 tbsp. sweet basil seeds
8 glasses (6 cups) milk
1 stick of cinnamon
8 green cardamoms
12 tsp. sugar (reduce or increase according to taste)

Preparation

Clean, wash and soak the sweet basil seeds in 2 cups of cold water for 2 hours. The seeds should have swollen and become fluffy-white by this time.

Slowly, on low heat, bring the milk to boil with the cinnamon and crushed cardamoms. Add the sugar. Boil for 10 minutes. Allow to cool and stir in the basil seeds with the water in which they had been soaked. Serve chilled.

Sadr-E-Kaanz
(Fermented Rice-Water)

This non-alcoholic drink is supposed to be very good for a sluggish liver. At one time it was even prescribed as treatment for jaundice. A glassful added to fish curry will give it an appetizing flavor. You will need a large earthenware pot to prepare sadr-e-kaanz. Fill it with water and after half an hour throw away the water and let the jar dry out.

Ingredients (Makes about 10 litres)

2 pounds (32 ounces) paddy (unhusked rice). Roast and grind coarsely.
A large bunch sour grapes
A fistful of mustard seed
4 tsp. thyme seed, crushed

Preparation

Put all the ingredients into the jar. Pour in 9 cups of boiling water and cover with a lid. Leave in a warm place. Over the next seven days, keep adding about 3 cups of the water in which you boil the rice for the morning and evening meals. On the eighth day the sadr-e-kaanz is ready to be consumed. Strain and serve cold.

Snacks and Tea-time Savouries

Kashmiris concentrate on two large meals a day. Breakfast generally consists of tea and fresh unleavened bread bought from the baker. The baker is an institution of great importance in Kashmir as the large variety of breads that are eaten at breakfast and tea-time, all come fresh from his shop. There is a baker on every street, catering to this demand. Hence only a few snacks and tea-time savouries are prepared at home, which are given here.

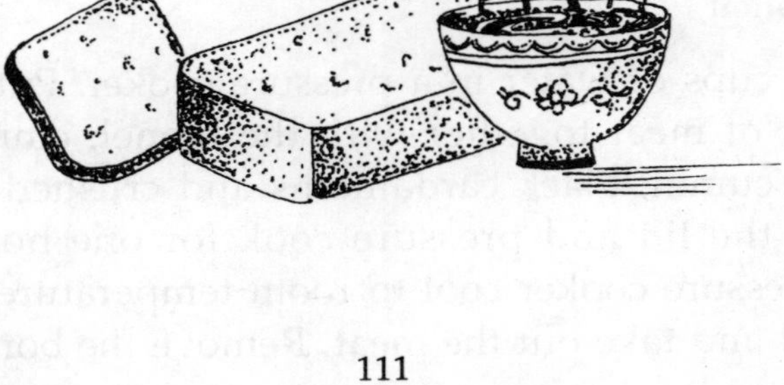

Hareesa
(Mince Paste Spread)

Hareesa is a winter-time breakfast dish and is eaten with oven-fresh flat bread bought from the corner baker's shop.

Ingredients (Serves 16)

2 pounds mutton — a whole chunk from the leg
4 tbsp. fennel seeds
1 stick cinnamom
1 tsp. white cumin
1 cup rice. Wash and soak for 4 hours.
7 black cardamoms
10 cloves garlic, crushed
2 medium-sized onions, sliced and divided
1 whole dry shallot, sliced
2 cups milk
½ tsp. saffron, soaked in a little warm water
15 green cardamoms
½ tsp. black cumin

Preparation

Boil 4 cups of water in a pressure cooker. Put in the chunk of meat together with the fennel, cinnamon, white cumin, black cardamoms and crushed garlic. Close the lid and pressure cook for one hour. Let the pressure cooker cool to room temperature. Open the lid and take out the meat. Remove the bones and keep the very tender meat aside. Strain the gravy and pour it back into the pressure cooker together with the soaked rice. Pressure cook for 20 minutes. Cool the cooker to room temperature. The rice should have been cooked to a soft mess. Put in the meat and beat and mash the mixture vigorously with a long-handled wooden ladle, till it becomes a sticky paste, the meat and rice completely homogenised. This takes some time — about 10 minutes of constant beating and mashing to make the Hareesa. Heat ¾ cup of oil. When it smokes, put in the sliced onion and shallot. Stir-fry till rich brown in color. Pour the sizzling hot oil over the Hareesa. Put the vessel back on the heat. Stir in two cups of milk, mixing it in thoroughly. Finally put in the saffron, crushed green cardamoms and black cumin. Serve hot.

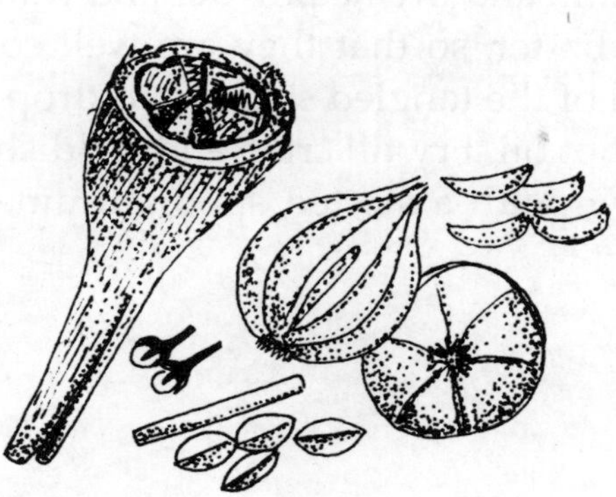

NADUR MONJI
(Lotus Root Fries)

Ingredients (Serves 4)

1 long, thick lotus root. Cut into 5 cm lengths, and quarter to form strips
2 cups oil
½ cup rice flour
½ tsp. salt
½ tsp. red chili powder or a little edible red food coloring
¼ tsp. black cumin
¼ tsp. powdered dry thyme seeds
A little water

Preparation

Thoroughly wash the lotus root strips, drain and pat dry. Heat the oil. Meanwhile make a thin batter with the rice flour, salt, chili powder (or edible red food coloring), cumin and thyme powder and water. Dip the strips in the batter, so that they are well coated. Pick up a handful of the tangled strips, and drop them into the sizzling hot oil. Fry till crisp and reddish brown in color. Remove with a slotted spoon, drain and serve hot.

Gaari Poor

(Water-Chestnut Flour Cookies)

Ingredients (Serves 10)

2 cups water-chestnut flour
1 pinch baking soda
1 cup ghee, divided
½ cup sugar
½ cup milk

Preparation

Sieve the flour and baking soda together. Rub 2 tbsp. ghee into the flour. Dissolve the sugar in the milk, warming it a little. Pour on the flour and knead it to form a soft dough. Divide in about 10 portions. Form each into a ball and roll out into a 7 cm diameter cookie. Deep fry in remaining ghee on medium heat till a rich brown in colour on each side. Drain, using a slotted spoon and serve piping hot.

THSUR TSOT
(Rice Flour Pancakes)

Ingredients (Serves 8)

1 cup rice flour
½ tsp. salt
¼ tsp. cumin seed
2 cups or enough cold water to make a thin custard-like batter
8 tbsp. oil

Preparation

Sieve the rice flour and put into a bowl. Add salt and cumin seed. Stir in the water gradually. Whisk to make a smooth paste. Cover and keep aside for half an hour.

Heat a griddle. Pour 1 tbsp. of oil on it. When it begins to smoke, pour 3 tbsp. of batter on it, tilting and turning the griddle, so that the batter spreads and thinly coats it. Cover with a lid and cook one high heat for one minute or till one side is slightiy browned. Remove the lid. Turn the pancake and cook on the other side. Serve hot.

Dub Maha
(Black Beans)

Ingredients (Serves 10-12)

2 pounds small black beans, cleaned and soaked in water overnight
1 tsp. turmeric
2 tsp. ginger powder
3 cloves
Salt and pepper to taste
2 tbsp. ghee or oil
1 onion, sliced fine
½ inch cube green ginger, sliced fine
4 cloves garlic, crushed
2 tsps. red chili powder
½ tsp. black cumin

Preparation

Cook the soaked beans in 6 cups of water with the turmeric powder, ginger powder, cloves and salt till soft and the water completely absorbed. The beans must not be broken. Heat the ghee/oil. Put in the onions and fry them till they are lightly browned, add the ginger and garlic. Stir-fry for 3 minutes. Stir in the chili powder and cumin and immediately after, the cooked beans. Stir well till all the moisture evaporates, but take care not to crush the beans. This dish has no gravy at all and is eaten as a snack with bread or naan.

Nadur Churma
(Lotus Stem Fries)

Ingredients (Serves 4)

¾ cup oil

1 long lotus-stem. Scrape clean, cut into 4 cm lengths and quarter them. Wash thoroughly and drain. Pat dry.

Salt and red chili powder to taste

Preparation

Heat the oil in a deep frying pan. When sizzling hot, put in the lotus stem strips in batches and fry till light brown, turning frequently. Remove with a slotted spoon and spread on a sheet of paper so that excess oil is absorbed and the strips remain crisp and dry. Sprinkle salt and chili powder and mix thoroughly. They are ready to serve.

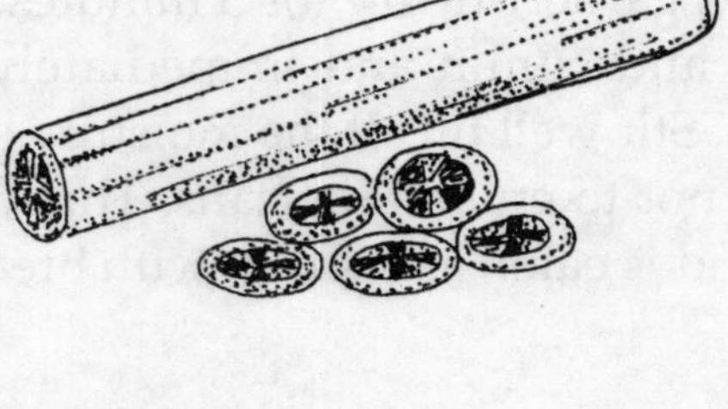

Yaji
(Rice Flour Cookies)

Ingredients (Makes 8)

2 cups rice flour
½ tsp. salt
1 tsp. cumin
4 walnuts, roughly chopped
A little water to knead the flour
1 tbsp. oil
1 cup water

Preparation

Traditionally an earthenware vessel with a lid was used to make this snack, but a pressure cooker will do very well.

Sieve the rice flour and salt together. Add the crushed cumin and walnuts and knead with a little water to make a soft dough. Divide into 8 portions and form into balls. Take a ball in your left hand and press the center to make a hollow, shaping it into a cup-like form. Heat oil in the vessel. When sizzling, add one cup of water. Just when it begins to boil, gently place the inverted cup-shaped cookies in the shallow liquid. Cover and allow to steam till the liquid evaporates completely and the rim of the hollow cookies is golden and crisp. Serve warm.

Chutneys and Pickles

CHUTNEYS

The special feature of chutneys in Kashmir is their use of yoghurt as the base. Some of these chutneys, therefore, appear like cottage cheese dips, using herbs and other ingredients to give each one a distinctive taste and flavor. The basic recipe is this. Tie 1½ cups of yoghurt in a piece of muslin and hang up to squeeze out water for 2 hours. The creamy cheese thus obtained is the basic ingredient. The following are the different chutneys that can be made with it.

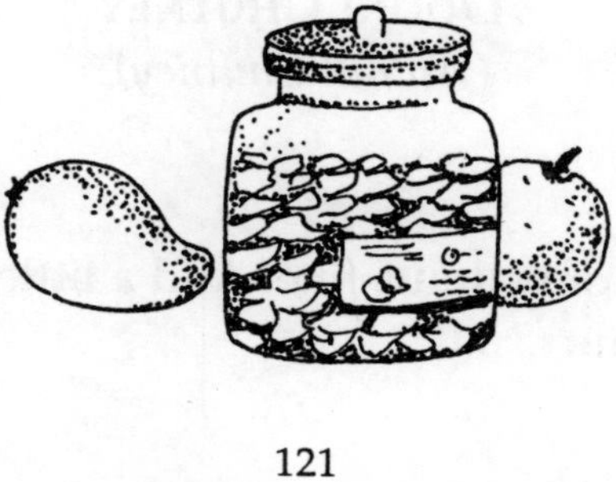

PUDINA CHUTNEY
(Mint Chutney)

Grind to a fine paste, ½ cup of fresh mint and 2 green chilies with salt to taste. Stir into the creamy, thick yoghurt.

MARTSAWANGAN CHUTNEY
(Green Chilies Chutney)

Green chilies, ground fine, with a little salt, will make the hot, flavorsome martsawangan chutney.

DOONI CHUTNEY
(Walnut Chutney)

Grind ¾ cup of walnuts fine. Add a little salt, and mix into the yoghurt.

ALA CHUTNEY
(Pumpkin Chutney)

½ lb. pumpkin, shredded fine. Simmer without adding any water till tender. Stir in 3 tbsp. of honey and a few raisins. Add a little yoghurt to make a thick, creamy chutney.

PICKLES

A variety of vegetables is pickled in Kashmir. These include kohlrabi, lotus stem, carrots, radish, peppers (green and red), garlic, onions, cabbage and eggplant. The special feature of these pickles is that no vinegar or lemon is used in their preparation. Mustard is used instead as a fermenting agent and they are mixed in mustard oil. Kashmiri pickles are hot and they keep for months, even a whole year. The basic recipe is as follows.

MONJI ANCHAR
(Kohlrabi Pickle)

Ingredients

4 pounds large, firm kohlrabi. Do not peel. Wash and dice into 1 inch cubes. Break the leaves into two and press between palms to soften a little. Spread out on a clean sheet and leave to dry overnight.

1 pound fresh green and red peppers. Break each into two and leave overnight spread on the sheet along with the kohlrabi.

2 tsp. ginger powder
1/3 cup red chili powder
1 tsp. thyme. Grind coarsely.
3 tbsp. mustard seeds. Crush coarsely.
1 cup mustard oil
4 tsp salt
1¼ tsp. cumin

Preparation

You will need a large basin. Mix all the ingredients thoroughly with both hands, rubbing the oil and spices into the kohlrabi cubes, leaves and peppers. Take a clean, dry jar and put the mixture into it, pressing it down so that the contents pack the jar fully, leaving no space for any air to be trapped inside. Close with a tight-fitting lid, ensuring that it is air-tight.

Place the jar in a tray to catch any overflow of oil. Leave it in a sunny place for about ten days. (Kashmiris make their pickles in late autumn when the weather is just perfect — neither too warm nor too cold.) Do not forget to bring the jar in after sunset every day. At the end of ten days the oil should have risen to the top, saturating the contents. The pickle is ready.

While serving, care should be taken to use only a clean, dry spoon, otherwise the pickle might spoil. A little oil can be poured in if the contents appear to be too dry. Store in a cool, dry place and the pickle will keep for months.

Pickles using other vegetables are also prepared according to this very basic recipe. Just ensure that the vegetables are as dry as possible before being pickled.

Spice Cakes

There are two kinds of spice-condiment cakes that Kashmiris make: one which uses the strong flavor of shallot and garlic and the other which uses that of asafoetida. Traditionally, the Muslims use the former, while the Pandits the latter. The cakes are prepared on a large scale and dried in the sun. They keep well for at least 6 months and can be used as required, throughout the year.

Garlic Flavored Vari Masala

(Spice Cake)

Ingredients

2 cloves garlic
1 tbsp. dried shallots
2 pounds dry red chilies (de-seeded)
2 tbsp. dry ginger (freshly ground and sieved)
1 tbsp. black cardamom seeds
6 cloves
2 tsp. white cumin
1 stick cinnamon
1 tsp. black cumin
½ cup coriander seeds
(Roast slightly just before grinding)
1 tbsp. saffron, crisped slightly on a warm griddle or tawa
1 betel nut
2 flower heads of cockscomb, crushed
2 tbsp. oil
4 betel leaves

Preparation

Grind the cleaned, peeled cloves of garlic and shallot to a paste. Keep covered in an earthenware bowl to mature for one day. On the next day, grind together the garlic-shallot paste, red chilies and all the spices to make as fine a paste as possible. Knead with a little oil. Form into balls and flatten with the hands to make 2 cm thick flat cakes. Pierce a hole in the middle of each cake with a finger and place on a plank of wood lined with large leaves to dry in the sun.

ASAFOETIDA-FLAVOURED VARI MASALA

The process and ingredients are the same, except that no garlic or shallot is used. Asafoetida is used instead. Soak 1 tbsp. of asafoetida in half a cup of water. When dissolved, bring to a boil. Use this liquid and the oil to mix the ingredients together and knead them.

GARAM MASALA

Ingredients

½ tsp. sugar
½ tsp. white zeera
2 black cardamoms
4 green cardamoms
½ tsp. ground cinnamon powder or 1 large stick
3 freshly roasted claves

Preparation

Grind all the ingredients to a fine powder.